THE SCIENCE AND TECHNOLOGY OF

Leonardo da Vinci

ELIZABETH
PAGEL-HOGAN

ILLUSTRATED BY
MICAH RAUCH

Titles in the **Build It Yourself Science Biographies** Set

Check out more titles at www.nomadpress.net

Nomad Press

A division of Nomad Communications

10 9 8 7 6 5 4 3 2 1

This book was manufactured by CGB Printers,
North Mankato, Minnesota, United States
May 2021, Job #1018286
ISBN Softcover: 978-1-64741-014-8
ISBN Hardcover: 978-164741-011-7

Educational Consultant, Marla Conn

Questions regarding the ordering of this book should be addressed to
Nomad Press
PO Box 1036, Norwich, VT 05055
www.nomadpress.net

Printed in the United States.

CONTENTS

Interested in Primary Sources? Look for this icon.

Use a smartphone or tablet app to scan the QR code and explore more! Photos are also primary sources because a photograph takes a picture at the moment something happens. You can find a list of URLs on the Resources page. If the QR code doesn't work, try searching the internet with the Keyword Prompts to find other helpful sources.

🔎 Leonardo da Vinci

1452: Leonardo da Vinci is born on April 15 in the town of Vinci in Florence, Italy.

1467: Leonardo apprentices at Andrea del Verrocchio's workshop in Florence.

1482: Leonardo moves to Milan, Italy. He begins keeping his famous notebooks.

1485: Leonardo makes the first sketches for inventions such as a flying machine, a tank, and a giant crossbow.

1488: Leonardo designs the viola organista.

1490: Leonardo begins work on a bronze horse statue for the duke of Sforza.

1490: Leonardo draws *Vitruvian Man*. Artist and pupil Salai moves in with Leonardo.

1493: Leonardo sketches ideas for an aerial screw, a possible precursor to a helicopter.

1495: Leonardo begins *The Last Supper*. It will take him two years to paint.

1496: Leonardo draws the three-dimensional shape models for his friend Luca Pacioli.

1497: Leonardo finishes the painting *The Last Supper*.

1498: Leonardo sketches a flying machine in his notebook.

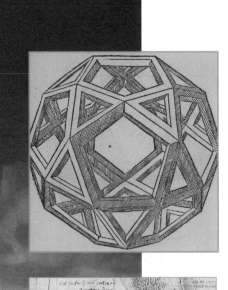

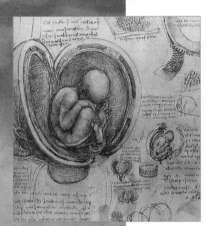

1500: Leonardo returns to Florence. His father dies four years later.

1502: Leonardo begins sketching the Golden Horn Bridge, a single-span bridge across the Horn River.

1502: Leonardo begins working for Cesare Borgia as a military engineer.

1503: Leonardo begins one of his most famous paintings, the *Mona Lisa*. He likely works on this painting during the course of several years and it is still in his studio when he dies. The *Mona Lisa* now hangs in the Louvre Museum in Paris, France.

1505: Leonardo returns to studying flight, but he is never able to create a self-propelled human flying machine.

1507: Leonardo's uncle Francesco dies and leaves his estate to Leonardo.

1508: Leonardo studies anatomy again. He visits the Santa Maria Nuova Hospital in Florence at night.

1513: Leonardo moves to Rome, Italy, to work for a new patron.

1516: Leonardo moves to France at the invitation of King Francis I.

1519: Leonardo dies in Cloux, France, at age 67.

MEET LEONARDO
DA VINCI

Even though Leonardo da Vinci (1452–1519) lived more than 500 years ago, people are still building and using his inventions. Artists are still studying and learning from his paintings and drawings. In fact, he is one of the most respected artists and scientists in history.

Back in his own day, Leonardo was considered one of the most talented artists and inventors. This is quite an honor, considering Leonardo lived during the **Renaissance**, a time when many great artists and thinkers made their marks on the world. Michelangelo (1475–1564), Raphael (1483–1520), and other talented artists were also creating at this time. What made Leonardo so special? How did someone who didn't even go to school become one of the greatest artists and inventors of all time?

ESSENTIAL QUESTION

Why was the Renaissance a time of great art, invention, and discovery?

WORDS TO KNOW

Renaissance: the period in European history between the 1300s and 1700, which was marked by dramatic social, political, artistic, and scientific change.

technology: the tools, methods, and systems used to solve a problem or do work.

botany: the study of plants.

anatomy: the study of the bodies of humans, animals, and other living things.

astronomy: the study of the sun, moon, stars, planets, and space.

spiritual: relating to the mind and spirit instead of the physical world.

Middle Ages: the period of time between the end of the Roman Empire and the beginning of the Renaissance, from about 350 to 1450 CE. It is also called the Medieval Era.

CE: put after a date, CE stands for Common Era and counts up from zero. BCE stands for Before the Common Era and counts down to zero. These are non-religious terms that correspond to AD and BC. This book was printed in 2021 CE.

clergy: a priest, monk, minister, or other person ordained by the church.

priest: a member of the clergy in Christianity who leads religious services and performs rites.

monk: a man who lives in a religious community and devotes himself to prayer.

Leonardo wasn't rich and famous. He didn't have a lot of money to buy expensive equipment and supplies. Many people describe him as being a genius or having some kind of mysterious gift. But Leonardo's gift wasn't mysterious. Leonardo's secret was that he wanted to understand the world around him— he was extremely curious. This curiosity drove him to work hard to learn everything he could.

Leonardo did three important things that made him different from everyone else.

1. He was dedicated to observation.

2. He never stopped asking questions.

3. He used the power of imagination.

Do you know people who do these three things in today's world? After relying on religion for answers for hundreds of years, many people in Leonardo's time were just starting to be aware of how much there was to learn about the world. How might Leonardo's life and work have been different had he been born during a different era? To answer that question, let's take a closer look at the Renaissance.

A statue of Leonardo da Vinci

Four Male Saints
from the workshop
of Fra Filippo Lippi

WELCOME TO THE RENAISSANCE

Leonardo lived during the Renaissance, a time from about 1300 through the 1600s. During this era, learning and ideas and inventions exploded all across Europe, beginning in Italy. All of this knowledge and discovery was related. Advances in mathematics improved art. Advances in **technology** improved daily life. New discoveries in science, in the fields of **botany, anatomy,** and **astronomy,** made people think differently about the church and their own **spiritual** lives.

Why was the Renaissance a time of so much learning?

The time before the Renaissance is called the **Middle Ages**. The Middle Ages lasted from about 350 to 1450 **CE**. In Europe during the Middle Ages, only a small number of people were educated. Education was usually offered only to the **clergy,** such as **priests** and **monks**. People still studied science, math, and medicine, but they learned about ideas that today we know to be incorrect.

3

WORDS TO KNOW

scholar: a person who studies a subject for a long time and knows a lot about it.

scroll: a piece of paper or parchment with writing on it that is rolled up into the shape of a tube.

prosperous: financially successful, wealthy.

sculpture: a carving of stone or metal.

engineering: the use of science, math, and creativity in the design and construction of things.

innovation: a new invention or way of doing something.

humanism: a belief that human beings can improve themselves and their world through a rational approach to problem-solving.

printing press: a machine that presses inked type onto paper.

moveable type: an important advance in printing where individual characters could be rearranged easily, allowing books to be printed more cheaply.

fossil: the remains of any living thing, including animals and plants, that have been preserved in rock.

Then, in 1453, a city called Constantinople was overrun by the Ottoman Turk army. Many of the **scholars** who lived in Constantinople fled to Italy. They brought books and **scrolls** and ideas with them. This time is usually considered the start of the Renaissance. The Renaissance was a time of learning and growth in art, technology, science, and literature. People shared information, learned new ideas, and the culture of Europe changed. It's appropriate, then, that the word *renaissance* means "rebirth."

The Renaissance was especially apparent in Florence, Italy. This is the same city where Leonardo da Vinci began his work. The city was **prosperous** and there was a lot of work for craftspeople. Florence was ruled by a small local government. The wealthy family in charge of Florence, the Medici, paid for lots of paintings, **sculptures**, and beautiful buildings. Other wealthy families did the same.

The dome of the Santa Maria del Fiore cathedral in Florence, Italy, designed by Filippo Brunelleschi (1377–1446). It is a symbol of the Renaissance and the **engineering** and architectural **innovations** that bloomed during this time.

During the Renaissance, there was also a new focus on an idea called **humanism**. The human mind could think through, or reason out, any problem. Renaissance leaders encouraged people to be creative and to think for themselves. Instead of relying on what religion claimed was true, people could observe the world and test out their own ideas. This was a big change from the Middle Ages.

Humanism is the idea that the HUMAN MIND has EXTRAORDINARY ABILITIES.

One major step that happened during the Renaissance was the invention of the **printing press**. This made it possible for multiple copies of books to be printed quickly so that knowledge could spread among the people. Can you imagine a world in which books were so rare, most people went their entire lives without ever seeing one, never mind reading one? Once Johannes Gutenberg (c. 1400–1468) introduced mechanical **moveable type** to Europe, more and more people had access to books, and therefore to the ideas and discoveries that were changing the course of humanity.

The Renaissance was the perfect time period for a person such as Leonardo. He was interested in everything and had a wide variety of skills. He studied the plants of the earth and the stars in the sky. He studied birds, **fossils**, wind, water, horses, human anatomy, Latin, music, and engineering.

WORDS TO KNOW

apprentice: a person who works with a master to learn a skill or trade.

optics: the study of the properties and behavior of light.

geometry: a branch of mathematics that deals with points, lines, and shapes and where they are in space.

engineer: someone who uses math, science, and creativity to solve problems or meet human needs.

mathematician: someone who studies mathematics, or numbers.

engineering design: the process engineers use to identify problems and come up with solutions.

portrait: a painting of a person showing only the head or head and shoulders.

will: a legal document that explains what happens to a person's belongings when they die.

dissect: to cut something apart to study what is inside.

LEONARDO'S LIFE

Leonardo was born in 1452 in a small town called Vinci. His name means "Leonardo of Vinci." His father, Piero da Vinci (1426–1504), and his mother, Caterina di Meo Lippi (1437–1493), were not married, which was frowned upon at the time.

Leonardo grew up in the country on his grandfather's farm. When he was about 13 years old, his father took him to the big city of Florence and got him a job as an **apprentice** in the workshop of Andrea del Verrocchio (1435–1488), a famous painter and sculptor. In 1472, when Leonardo was 20, he got his own studio in Florence. But he didn't have a lot of success there.

In 1482, he moved to Milan, another city in Italy. There, he met with famous scholars who studied **optics** and **geometry**. He became an **engineer** and opened his own workshop. He put on fantastic theater performances and had his own vineyard.

While in Milan, he painted *The Last Supper*, which is now a very famous work of art. He also adopted a boy he nicknamed "Salai" (1480–1524), or "Little Devil." Salai was his assistant, a pupil, and a companion for more than 30 years. Salai stole from Leonardo and from Leonardo's friends. He also broke things and didn't have good manners. Despite this bad behavior, Leonardo loved him.

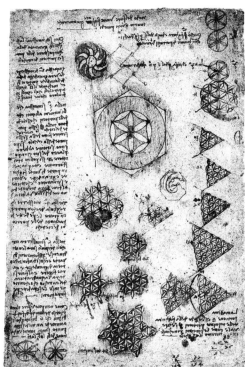

Leonardo was always fascinated with geometry. He drew this sometime between 1478 and 1519.

This **portrait** is of Francesco Melzi, painted c. 1510–1511.

Credit: Giovanni Antonio Boltraffio

In 1500, after 18 years in Milan, Leonardo had to flee the city when the French army invaded. Leonardo packed up his thousands of notebook pages. With Salai and his friend Luca Pacioli (1447–1517), a **mathematician**, Leonardo roamed around Italy for a long time—19 years!

Leonardo spent a short time working for Cesare Borgia (1475–1507), a powerful military leader. Borgia wanted Leonardo to make weapons for war. Leonardo loved **engineering design**, and he needed the work. But Borgia was cruel, and Leonardo soon stopped working for him.

When Leonardo's father died in 1504, Leonardo didn't receive any money or land in his father's **will**. He was still looking for a home. Leonardo did a little bit of work for the French king, Louis XII, who lived in Milan. It was around this time that Leonardo met Francesco Melzi (1491–1570). Melzi was 17 years old and wanted to be an artist. He became Leonardo's student and companion for the rest of Leonardo's life.

In 1503, Leonardo started painting the *Mona Lisa*. He worked on this painting for 13 YEARS!

What made Leonardo a genius? His drive to know all about everything was a huge part of the way he learned. **Learn more in this video.**

PBS Leonardo *Mona Lisa*

PS

Leonardo moved to Rome in 1513. He worked for the pope, the leader of the Catholic Church, and continued his studies in anatomy and nature. But even though he had permission to **dissect** human bodies, some people thought he was calling up evil spirits. He was no longer allowed to study anatomy.

In 1517, Leonardo took his notebooks and left Italy for good. The young French king, Francis I, had met Leonardo in 1515, when Leonardo had made a mechanical lion that walked—the king thought Leonardo was a genius. The king wanted Leonardo to come to his court so they could talk about anything and everything.

Leonardo was called the "Premier Painter, Engineer, and Architect of the King." King Francis I gave Leonardo a home, called Clos Luce. An underground tunnel connected the king's palace to Leonardo's house. Of course, Melzi came with Leonardo. Leonardo continued painting, thinking, dreaming, and writing in his notebooks.

In 1519, Leonardo died in France. He gave Salai part of a vineyard. He gave his housekeeper a fur coat. And he left everything else, including his incredible notebooks, to Melzi.

Leonardo da Vinci, a presumed self-portrait, c. 1512

WRITE IT DOWN

One of the most incredible things Leonardo created was his collection of notebooks. He started drawing and writing in a notebook when he was a child and continued this practice all of his life. More than 7,200 pages of his notebooks are preserved, but scholars believe that is probably only one-quarter of all the notebooks he created. Leonardo put all of his thoughts, questions, ideas, designs, and sketches into the pages of those books.

He didn't separate things into different subjects or chapters in his notebooks. During the Renaissance, information wasn't divided into different subjects as it is today. People such as Leonardo explored many different subjects and many times ideas overlapped different topics. Leonardo made connections between all of his interests. Math and anatomy influenced his art. He used art to improve his engineering. He studied engineering to better understand human anatomy. In Leonardo's mind, everything was connected.

A page from one of Leonardo's notebooks
Credit: Wellcome Collection (CC BY 4.0)

Freedom

Growing up, Leonardo lived with many different family members. His mother and father were not married. In Italy during the 1400s, that was a big problem. It was not considered respectable to be born to unmarried parents. It even meant Leonardo could not have the same job as his father and he could not attend schools and universities. This could have limited Leonardo's future. Instead, it released Leonardo to explore all of the subjects that interested him. It also freed him to come up with his own questions and ideas about the world. Why might it be easier to follow your own passions if you aren't expected to go to school or work with a family member?

WORDS TO KNOW

zibaldone: one of Leonardo's notebooks, or a collection of different kinds of things.

What can we learn from Leonardo today? Plenty of things! In this book, we'll explore Leonardo's inventions, designs, art, and scientific observations. You'll discover the connections that Leonardo made as he worked to improve his own mind and try to find connections yourself. Many of the projects in this book explore more than one concept or skill. Look for patterns and new ways of thinking about things.

Good Science Practices

Every good scientist keeps a science journal!

Scientists use the scientific method to keep their experiments organized. Choose a notebook to use as your science journal. As you read through this book and do the activities, keep track of your observations and record each step in a scientific method worksheet, like the one shown here.

Question: What are we trying to find out? What problem are we trying to solve?

Research: What is already known about the problem?

Hypothesis/Prediction: What do we think the answer will be?

Equipment: What supplies are we using?

Method: What procedure are we following?

Results: What happened? Why?

Each chapter of this book begins with an essential question to help guide your exploration of Leonardo da Vinci and his work. Keep the question in your mind as you read the chapter. At the end of each chapter, use your science journal to record your thoughts and answers.

ESSENTIAL QUESTION

Why was the Renaissance a time of great art, invention, and discovery?

MAKE YOUR OWN
ZIBALDONE

INVENTOR KIT

- paper (any kind! Look for scrap, colored, lined, etc.)
- cardboard (such as a cereal or snack box)
- duct tape
- binder ring
- string or lanyard

A **zibaldone** is the Italian word for "a heap of things." This is what Leonardo's notebook was called. He collected a heap of ideas, observations, questions, and experiments on the pages of his notebooks, putting everything he saw or thought into the same book, instead of having different notebooks for different topics. And he used every corner and both sides of every page. In the 1400s, books and paper were more plentiful than they had ever been, but they still weren't as inexpensive as they are today! As you explore and observe the world through Leonardo's eyes, you need a notebook to record your ideas. Make your own zibaldone!

❯ **Using scissors, trim your pieces of paper so they are all the same size.** Stack all of the sheets together. Staple them along the longer side. Don't use too much paper or it will be too thick to staple. A good size is something you can hold in one hand while drawing in it with the other hand.

❯ **Wrap the cardboard around your paper, inside out so the covers are blank.** Trim your cardboard to be about a half-inch larger than your paper.

❯ **Staple the cardboard and paper together along the spine, or the fold, so the paper is secured.** Put a strip of duct tape along the spine of the book to cover the staples.

❯ **Use a hole punch to punch a hole in the top, left-hand corner of the cardboard.**

❯ **Secure the binder ring through the hole and attach the string or lanyard to the ring.** Now, you can wear the notebook on your belt, just as Leonardo did.

❯ **Decorate the cover of your zibaldone.** Remember, paper was valuable in Leonardo's time, so try to use all corners, spaces, and sides of the paper!

Think Like Leo!

Leonardo asked questions all the time. How does the frog jump? What makes the water in the stream move? Come up with 10 questions about the world around you. List these questions in your zibaldone and draw and write any observations that might answer these questions.

TEXT TO **WORLD**

Do you keep a journal? Do you post on a blog? How is this similar to Leonardo's notebooks?

Chapter 1

LEONARDO'S
ART

YOU'RE THAT REALLY GOOD ARTIST EVERYONE IS TALKING ABOUT! LEONARDO DA VINCI, RIGHT?

I AM! DO YOU HAVE AN INTEREST IN THE ARTS?

I THINK I WANT TO BECOME AN ARTIST ONE DAY, TOO.

Ask someone who Leonardo da Vinci was, and they will probably mention his most famous painting, the *Mona Lisa*. They may also mention *The Last Supper*, another of his famous paintings. Leonardo da Vinci is very well known as a painter.

ESSENTIAL QUESTION

How did Leonardo's view of the world influence his paintings and drawings?

Interestingly, while most people know of Leonardo da Vinci as an incredible artist, Leonardo didn't actually describe himself as an artist. In fact, when he wrote a letter introducing himself to the duke of Milan, he said, "In painting, I can do everything possible, as well as any other man."

That was an **understatement**. Maybe even a lie! When it came to painting, Leonardo may have been better than any other man. He also changed the way artists created art.

CHILDHOOD ART

Leonardo grew up in the Italian countryside outside of the city of Florence. Even though there were schools in Florence, Leonardo was not welcome. Since his parents were not married when he was born, Leonardo was considered **illegitimate**. Illegitimate children were not permitted in schools.

WHY DOESN'T *Mona Lisa* **HAVE EYEBROWS?** Historians think the original did have eyebrows, but when the painting was cleaned, his thin layer of brushstrokes were wiped away.

Instead of studying in a classroom, Leonardo spent his days outdoors. His school was nature and his family's farm. That's where he learned about plants and herbs. He studied streams and waterfalls and noted the weather. He learned about the animals of the countryside, from worms and lizards to birds and horses.

WORDS TO KNOW

notary: a person who handles legal papers such as contracts and deeds.

mirror writing: backward writing that goes from right to left.

ambidextrous: able to use the right and left hands equally well.

hatch marks: lines drawn close together to create areas of shadow in a drawing.

But he didn't simply observe the world around him—he captured what he saw in sketches and notes in his notebooks. Even as a child, Leonardo drew what he saw in the land around his home. Stories say Leonardo carried a drawing pad with him everywhere. This might not seem unusual today, but in the 1400s, it was very rare for a child to have a pencil and paper.

Leonardo had access to pencils and paper because his father and grandfather were both **notaries**. A notary handled business contracts, wills, and legal documents. This meant there was paper and pencils around the house.

His family noticed his artistic skill, and when Leonardo was 14 years old, his father got him a position as an apprentice with an artist in Florence. The artist was Andrea del Verrocchio (1435–1488).

In Verrocchio's workshop, Leonardo's talent for art flourished. Here, he learned how to create all kinds of products, such as paintings, sculptures, musical instruments, and more. He also learned how to make paint, clean brushes, transfer drawings, paint on wood, and carve stone. Leonardo worked hard and honed his skill. Soon he was allowed to finish paintings, a privilege reserved for the most experienced students.

Leonardo's hometown

Mirror Writing

Leonardo was left-handed. Sometimes, people forced left-handed children to use their right hands, but Leonardo had always been allowed to write with his left hand. Sometimes, he wrote backward from right to left in his notebooks. This is called **mirror writing**. Some people said Leonardo wrote in mirror writing to hide his ideas in code, but some of today's biographers think it was simply to prevent the ink from smearing on the page. He could also write from left to right when he needed other people to read his writing, such as when he wrote letters. So, Leonardo was probably **ambidextrous**, or able to write and draw with both hands.

THE DRAGON SHIELD

As Leonardo studied technique and grew more accomplished in his art, he still loved combining ideas from his imagination with real elements from nature.

One day, while Leonardo was still an apprentice, his father brought him a shield to paint for a local man from Vinci. Leonardo wasn't going to paint just an ordinary shield. He was going to make something fantastic. Leonardo turned to nature for materials to make his creation. He collected parts of real animals and insects, including lizards, crickets, snakes, butterflies, and bats. Then, he reassembled the body parts to create a horrifying imaginary creature. People often describe the creature as a dragon.

LEONARDO NEVER SIGNED HIS WORKS. He also never kept a record or list of them. This can make it hard to know which paintings and drawings are really his. One of the ways art experts verify if a work is actually Leonardo's is to look for his signature left-handed **hatch marks.**

WORDS TO KNOW

ducat: a gold coin used during the Renaissance in Europe.

portray: to describe or depict someone or something.

depth: how deep something is, or the measurement that gives a shape **three-dimensional (3-D)** qualities.

three-dimensional (3-D): something that appears solid and can be measured in three directions, length, width, and depth.

As the story goes, when his father saw the terrifying beast, he jumped back in surprise. His father was impressed. His son's creation wasn't just a shield—it was a piece of art. He sold it for 100 **ducats** (about $15,000 today)! Leonardo's dad got a different, plainer shield for the man from Vinci. Sadly, images of the dragon have not survived the passage of time.

Leonardo had a keen eye for noticing detail in nature, but he also had a wonderful imagination that he used to create new things.

LEONARDO'S SIGNATURE STYLE

Leonardo learned many things as an apprentice in Verrocchio's workshop. One of the regular assignments for apprentice painters was to draw draped cloth. By drawing cloths over and over, apprentices learned to see and **portray** how light hits an object. They learned how to make something look real by representing **depth**. Adding light and shadow to create the ripples and folds in the cloth made it look more real and less like a flat picture.

Renaissance Careers

Artists during the Renaissance were more like tradespeople or crafters. Artists didn't create paintings or sculptures for museums or art galleries. They were businesspeople and made art to sell. Wealthy nobles would commission, or hire, artists to create beautiful pieces for their homes. Artists had workshops in cities where they painted, sculpted, and forged their creations. They took on apprentices, usually young men, and taught them the skills and techniques to create paintings or carvings. The apprentices would also clean the workshop and make or fix any supplies needed.

Look at the folds of cloth in this painting, called *The Annunciation* (da Vinci and Verrocchio). What makes them look real?

Nature and the real world were sources of Leonardo's inspiration. He wanted his art to look as realistic as possible. He carefully studied the way light and shadows look in the real world.

Leonardo mastered the ability to show where light shone in his art. In drawing, he used curved hatch marks to create a rounded feeling to objects. In paintings, he used light layers of oil paint that made people appear to glow with life.

Look at the hatching lines Leonardo used to make this woman's face appear rounded. How did he create areas of light and shadow?

🔍 Leonardo life in drawing

PS

But Leonardo wasn't done innovating in art. He thought of other techniques as well. For example, artists such as Verrocchio painted people and objects with outlines. Outlines made things appear flat and unrealistic.

As a skilled observer of the real world, Leonardo knew there are no outlines around things. Leonardo developed a technique called **sfumato**. Sfumato is the Italian word for "smoke." It's a type of painting that blurs the edges of things and creates a smokiness in a painting.

Edges are hard to find in Leonardo's paintings. He used brushes and his fingertips to blur lines and blend colors together. With sfumato, his paintings looked more real, more alive than any others.

Take a look at this painting. Can you see the effect of sfumato?

USING OIL INSTEAD OF TEMPERA

What did you do if you were an artist in the 1400s and you needed more paint? There were no arts-and-crafts stores back then! All artists in the 1400s had to make their own paint. One of the jobs of the apprentice was to learn how to make **tempera** paint. Tempera is made from egg yolks. It dries fast. Tempera paint gets its colors from adding different ingredients, everything from flowers and spices to ground-up rocks and seashells. These items provide the **pigments**.

Leonardo loved to experiment, so when a new kind of oil-based paint became popular in the Netherlands, he was one of the first to try this new **medium**.

Oil paint is made from mixing pigments, the same kind used in tempera, with linseed oil. Oil paint dries slowly—Leonardo loved how it gave him time to apply small strokes and thin layers. In some paintings, scientists have found he applied 40 incredibly thin layers of paint!

Leonardo didn't make many sculptures, but here's a link to one he probably did make. The laughing baby is a familiar feature in his work. What else reminds you of Leonardo's style?

🔎 Leonardo's surviving sculpture

PS

THE LAST SUPPER

Leonardo loved to innovate. He loved trying new ways of doing things. Some say his paintings aren't works of art—instead, they are experiments, because they are examples of how he tried something new. Some of his innovations worked wonderfully. Some did not.

While he was staying with the duke of Milan, the duke asked Leonardo to paint a famous scene from the Bible. Leonardo started the painting in 1494. *The Last Supper* is a **mural**, which means it is painted on a wall inside the dining hall of a monastery. At this time, most artists used tempera to paint their murals. Murals were usually painted while the plaster was wet. Painting on wet plaster had to be done quickly, and it couldn't really be changed later.

This was not Leonardo's style. Leonardo liked to take his time. He liked to go back and change his art. So, he tried a new method. He decided to paint his mural on dry wall plaster. He used a mix of oil and tempera paints. He painted like he usually did—slowly. Some days, he painted without stopping, and some days he didn't paint at all. He just stood there, gazing at his painting, thinking. He might add one brushstroke or a thin coat of paint to develop layers of light and shadow.

It took him four years, but luckily for the duke and for Leonardo, he did finish this painting.

Unluckily, Leonardo's innovative technique of painting on dry plaster didn't succeed. After only 20 years, the paint started to flake off of the wall. After 200 years, the monks at the monastery thought the painting was so worthless they cut a doorway through the wall and chopped off part of the painting.

People often think of **ARTISTS AS WORKING ALONE,** but from the beginning, Leonardo worked with teams to produce his art and experiments.

THE PERFECTIONIST

Leonardo's first big job as an artist was to paint a large picture for a monastery near Florence. Unfortunately, he never finished the project. And this wasn't the first time. Eventually, Leonardo gained a reputation for not completing his work. Some people say it was because he was a **perfectionist**. A perfectionist wants everything to be perfect, without errors or mistakes. He had a vision in his mind of what he wanted his art to look like. When the work-in-progress didn't look like the image in his head, it upset him and he couldn't keep working on it.

Others say his vision for his work was overwhelming. He dreamed big and planned big, but when it came time to do the work, it was too much for him.

Makers Make Mistakes?

Leonardo was a maker. He loved to design and create. One thing that makers make is mistakes. If you want to try new things, innovate, invent, design, and create, you have to be ready to make mistakes. But Leonardo wasn't careless. He thought things through, tried them out, made detailed plans, and experimented. He then learned from his experiments, especially the mistakes. That's one of the reasons we still revere him today.

For instance, when he was painting the *Adoration of the Magi*, he planned for 60 people in the background. He wanted each person to look as though they were reacting to the other people—he didn't want them to repeat poses or movements. He also wanted the light to be reflecting accurately off of every object. He set himself a huge challenge. Maybe too big. Take a look at the unfinished painting here. Do you think the results match what Leonardo had envisioned?

Leonardo had so many ideas, so many things he was interested in, it was easy to become distracted.

THE *MONA LISA*

The *Mona Lisa* might be Leonardo's most famous painting. It is a portrait, or a painting of a person. Portraits usually include only the head and shoulders of a person.

WORDS TO KNOW

vellum: fine paper made from the skin of a calf.

forgery: a copy, not the original.

perspective: a skill used in drawing to give the correct view of objects in a painting, using their height, width, and position to each other. It can be used to create a sense of distance.

horizon: the line where earth and sky appear to meet.

Leonardo started painting the *Mona Lisa* in 1503 but didn't finish it until 1517. He kept working on it for 14 years, adding tiny strokes and very light layers of oil paint year after year. *Mona Lisa* is painted on a plank of wood, not a canvas. Take a look on page 13.

La Bella Principessa— Forgery or Masterpiece?

In 2007, an art collector saw a drawing of a woman, done in chalk on **vellum**, at a New York museum. The artist was unknown, but this collector was convinced it was Leonardo. For almost 10 years, experts in art, history, and even fingerprinting investigated the portrait. Some people are convinced it's by Leonardo, others think it's a **forgery**. No one knows for sure.

The *Mona Lisa* is a famous portrait for many reasons. One of the reasons is the mysterious smile on the face of the woman in the painting. People love guessing what she was thinking. The smile looks so real because of Leonardo's knowledge of the muscles of the human body. We'll learn more about Leonardo's interest in anatomy in Chapter 5.

Women in the Renaissance

Many skilled artists came from Florence, including women. Nelli (1524–1588) was a nun who lived and painted in Florence during Leonardo's time. She is considered the first female Renaissance painter from Florence. Nelli is one of a few women mentioned in a biography called *Lives of Artists* published in 1550, which also included Leonardo da Vinci and other famous artists such as Raphael (1483–1520) and Caravaggio (1571–1610). Other female artists mentioned in this book are Properzia de' Rossi (1490–1530), a famous sculptor, and Sofonisba Anguissola (1535–1625), who worked for the queen of Spain. Why might we know so much less about female artists than male artists?

Based on his knowledge of **perspective**, he painted the woman's eyes so that her left eye gazes at you, but her right eye gazes to the side. Leonardo knew this technique would make it seem as though she was watching viewers as they move in front of the painting.

Leonardo used sfumato expertly in the *Mona Lisa* to create blended shadows in the background. He also made the **horizon** line uneven behind her head. This helps give the painting more depth.

The *Mona Lisa* shows the skills and knowledge Leonardo acquired during years of studying art, human anatomy, and math.

Even though he didn't brag about himself as a painter, Leonardo valued painting. He argued it was more noble than poetry and more elevated than sculpture. The *Mona Lisa* was by his bedside when he died.

While Leonardo was known as a great painter—and still is—he was also an innovative engineer who thought up many designs. Some of those designs laid the foundation for things we use today. We'll find out more in the next chapter.

ESSENTIAL QUESTION

How did Leonardo's view of the world influence his paintings and drawings?

MAKE YOUR OWN
PIGMENT-COATED PAPER

INVENTOR KIT
° thick paper, such as card stock
° acrylic paint (black is easiest to see when you scratch it away)
° dish soap
° stylus (a toothpick works well)

During the 1400s, there were no ballpoint pens or mechanical pencils. Leonardo carried his notebooks everywhere, but he didn't carry a quill and pot of ink. He often used a metal stylus and scratched lines onto paper coated with a pigment.

> Mix a dab of your acrylic paint with a small amount of dish soap.

> Lay out newspapers so you don't get your work surface dirty. Cover your paper with the acrylic paint-dish soap mix and let it dry.

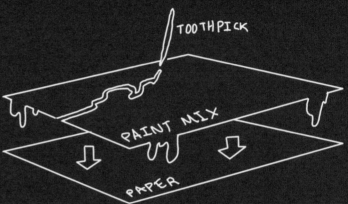

> Use the toothpick like a stylus and practice scratching away the paint. Try writing words and drawing things you see. How is scratching away a coating different from drawing or writing with ink?

The woman in the *Mona Lisa* is probably **LISA DEL GIOCONDO**, an Italian noblewoman. The name "**MONA**" is a contraction of "**MADONNA**," the term used to address an Italian lady. The painting is also called *La Gioconda*, a pun on the woman's last name.

Think Like Leo!

Leonardo used small lines, or hatch marks, in his art. Experiment with making small lines. Is it easier to draw light or shadow when using a stylus?

TEXT TO **WORLD**

Have you ever seen a painting by Leonardo da Vinci hanging in a museum or on the internet? What did it make you think of?

MIX IT UP
PAINT PIGMENT

Renaissance painters found and made their own paint pigments. Pigment is what gives paint its color. Add a lot of pigment and the color is richer and more intense. Add less, and the color is lighter.

❱ **Let your dirt and plants dry completely.**

❱ **Grind your dirt or plants into dust using your mortar and pestle or grind them between two rocks.** Make sure you grind your pigments over a piece of paper so you can collect the dust. This is your pigment!

❱ **Extract pigment from different things.** Try clay, bricks, dried fruit, or vegetables. How do the different types of pigment compare to each other?

❱ **Store your dry pigment in jars, bottles, or bags.** Add them to egg yolk for tempera painting as desired (see the next activity).

Think Like Leo!

Painters in the Renaissance often used limited sets of colors in their paintings. Why?

MAKE YOUR OWN
TEMPERA PAINT

Early Renaissance painters used egg tempera paint. The egg is a tempering, or binding, material that holds the colors together. Colors came from natural materials such as flowers, plants, rocks, and minerals.

Because egg tempera dries quickly, it had to be used immediately. It could not be stored and saved and used later. Every time an artist wanted to paint, they had to mix up a new batch of tempera paint. If they mixed too little paint, they couldn't be sure their next batch would match the color in their first batch. If they mixed too much, they wasted their expensive ingredients.

Luckily for Leonardo, oil paints became more available in the 1400s. Oil paints dried slower and could be saved and used later. Try making some of your own tempera paint!

❯ **Crack an egg over a bowl and separate the yolk from the white.** You can do this by slipping the yolk back and forth between the shell halves and letting the white fall into a bowl.

❯ **Place the yolk in another bowl and add food coloring or your pigments.** Stir with a spoon to mix it well.

❯ **Paint with your homemade egg tempera.** How is it different from other paints you've used? How quickly does it dry? How does this affect your painting?

❯ **Discard your paint when you are done painting.** You'll have to make a fresh batch the next time, just like Renaissance painters.

Think Like Leo!

Can you blend and overlap egg tempera colors? Test egg tempera on different kinds of paper. In your zibaldone, describe the differences. Does light reflect off dry egg tempera? Or does the paint absorb light? Is the dried paint shiny or more flat?

WORDS TO KNOW

tempering: to bind something together, as with pigment and egg yolk.

Chapter 2

CIVIL ENGINEERING: FROM BRIDGES
TO TANKS

In addition to being an artist, Leonardo was an engineer. Engineering is the design and creation of engines, machines, devices, and processes. Why do you think art and engineering were so strongly linked in Leonardo's mind?

When Leonardo was an apprentice to Verrocchio, artists were considered to be craftspeople. Artists weren't creating art for museums or galleries. They were making objects that people used every day. Art was beautiful, but it still had to be useful.

ESSENTIAL QUESTION

How does understanding the parts of a machine help you understand how the machine works?

Art and engineering were intertwined. Engineering was a way of applying art in the real world, and art was a way to make the machines and structures of daily life beautiful. Do you think this is still the case?

WORDS TO KNOW

device: a piece of equipment, such as a phone, that is made for a specific purpose.

process: an activity that takes several steps to complete.

sphere: a round, solid figure, a ball.

spire: a pointed roof, such as on a tower.

concave: a surface that curves inward, like the inside of a sphere.

pulley: a simple machine consisting of a wheel with a grooved rim that a rope or chain is pulled through to help lift a load.

hoist: a device that works with a pulley to lift heavy loads.

RAISE A SPHERE

One of Leonardo's earliest engineering projects was helping to put a huge golden **sphere** on top of the even larger dome of the cathedral in Florence. Leonardo was 19 years old when Verrocchio was hired to take on this project. The cathedral was already built, but the finishing touch had to be accomplished: the placing of the sphere. The sphere was a huge ball made of stone that weighed 2 tons, or 2,000 pounds.

Before the sphere went on top of the **spire**, it needed to be covered with eight sheets of thin copper. But how? Glue was not the answer. Could they melt the metal around the ball? There were no welding torches in the Renaissance.

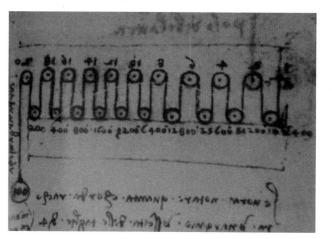

Leonardo's sketches of pulleys

Verrocchio and his apprentices, including Leonardo, used **concave** mirrors, each about 3 feet wide. The mirrors focused and aimed sunlight at the copper. The heat of the sunlight melted the copper sheets together around the sphere. Leonardo called these mirrors "fire mirrors" in his notebooks.

The architect of the dome, Filippo Brunelleschi (1377–1446), designed a system of **pulleys** and **hoists** to raise the heavy ball to the top of the dome. Leonardo made detailed drawings of these devices. He learned how they worked and recorded them in his notebooks. It was the first of his many hundreds of engineering designs.

The sphere on top of Brunelleschi's dome

Brunelleschi's Dome

Brunelleschi's dome crowns the top of the cathedral in Florence. It was designed by Filippo Brunelleschi and built during the 1430s. Like Leonardo, Brunelleschi studied a variety of subjects, from goldsmithing to architecture. Building the dome required the perfect combination of art, mathematics, and engineering. In fact, Brunelleschi invented some of the machines he used to build the dome. The dome is self-supporting, which means it holds itself up. There are almost 4 million bricks in the dome. It is still the largest brick dome in the world.

DRAWING MACHINES

The period of the Renaissance was filled with people making new discoveries and finding new ways of doing things. Leonardo was a leader among innovators back then. He loved experimenting, and the culture of the Renaissance encouraged people to be creative.

The fact that Leonardo drew machines wasn't that unusual. Many Renaissance "technologists" drew machines. But they drew them completely assembled. They drew the finished products.

Leonardo didn't do things the way other people did. Leonardo drew machines his own way, a new way. He drew things in their separate parts and pieces. He zoomed in on sections and enlarged small pieces. He drew **diagrams** of how the parts would fit together.

By drawing each piece separately, he could think about its movement and function. It was as though he were thinking out loud, but he did it with drawing. His artistic skill meant his drawings were detailed and accurate—his devices and inventions almost seem to move on the page.

Does today's culture value innovation?

MACHINES OF WAR

While the Renaissance was mostly a peaceful time, countries and nations still went to war. There was still a need for weapons. When Leonardo wrote his famous letter to the duke of Milan, he described all of his clever military inventions. The duke of Milan needed to prepare for war and Leonardo knew these things would interest him.

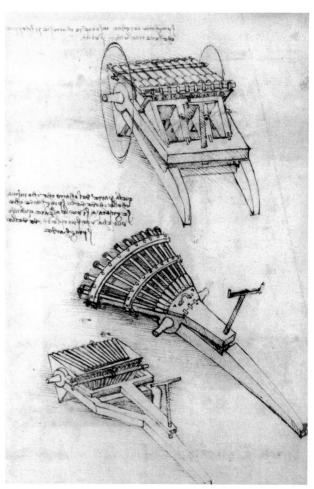

A sketch of a type of gun, fifteenth century

Leonardo promised that his ideas would help the duke defend his city. Leonardo mentioned bridges, cannons, chariots, catapults, ways to drain swamps and build tunnels, and "methods for destroying any fortress."

Leonardo hadn't actually built any of these things. His ideas only existed on paper, in his notebooks—they were only **theoretical**. But he didn't mention this to the duke. He wanted someone to help him pay for all of these spectacular machines and hoped the duke would be interested.

The duke was interested. He invited Leonardo to Milan.

Though Leonardo HATED LARGE-SCALE VIOLENCE, it was one of the only ways he could get support for his inventions.

The most famous of his theoretical designs was a giant crossbow. It was 80 feet across. His drawing of the crossbow is detailed, but he struggled with the mathematics. He thought if a person pulled the string back twice as far, it would send a **projectile**, such as a large arrow or cannonball, twice as far or twice as fast. But he wasn't quite right with his calculations, and he never got a chance to build his giant crossbow.

Leonardo also designed the first tank. His machine didn't look like modern tanks you might see on today's battlefields. Instead, it was a rolling cart filled with guns, more like an armored car with a domed cover. It looked more like a large turtle or hut moving along on wheels. It was never built—we have only his sketches.

Don't Mess with Leonardo's Design

In 2003, engineers in England tried to build Leonardo's giant crossbow. For its first attempt, the team decided to make some changes to Leonardo's design. The engineers faced many problems, including cracking wood and issues with the sling. When they tested the crossbow, the cannonballs flew only 25 yards. After adjustments, other tests sent the cannonball 50 yards. The team made a second crossbow and tried to stay true to Leonardo's designs. With the new designs, the crossbow shot a cannonball 60 yards. Then, the wood cracked and the device broke. Would you consider this experiment a success or a failure?

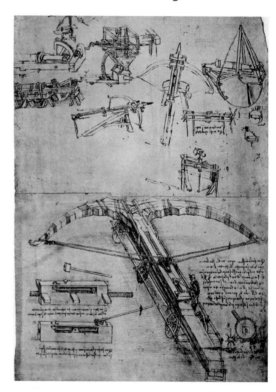

 You can see how some engineers tried to replicate Leonardo's design in this long video. The crossbow is one of the first devices discussed.

🔍 Leonardo's Dream Machines

Historians are baffled by a strange detail in Leonardo's instructions for building the tank. If the tank was built exactly as described in the directions, the front wheels would move in the opposite direction of the back wheels.

The tank would not go anywhere. Why would he design the tank this way? Was it a mistake? Or was it a trick?

Later in his life, Leonardo worked for Duke Cesare Borgia (1475–1507) for about eight months. Borgia was one of the most violent military leaders of his age.

A replica of Leonardo's tank, based on his drawings

Water Ways

Leonardo loved studying water. He also studied ways for people to stay underwater. He designed a very early version of scuba gear—a diving suit with a mask and a series of tubes that connected to the surface to allow a person to breathe. Leonardo thought these diving suits could help cities on the water defend themselves—but he also knew attackers could use these same plans to invade a city. So, he kept some of the design details secret and didn't write them in his notebook. "I do not wish to publish this because of the evil nature of men," he wrote, "who might use it for murder on the sea bed."

WORDS TO KNOW

suspension: to hang something in the air free on all sides except at the place where it is supported.

force: a push or pull on an object.

friction: the resistance caused when one object or surface moves against another.

gravity: the force that attracts one thing to another.

aerial: relating to the air.

revolution: one complete turn made by something moving in a circle around a fixed point.

One day, Borgia's army came to a river that was too wide to cross and there was no bridge. The only material nearby was cut wood. Leonardo designed and built a self-supporting bridge using the wood. There were no supports in the water or **suspension** wires. He laid the wood so that each piece held the weight of the other pieces. The **forces** of **friction** and **gravity** held the bridge together and the army was able to cross the river.

Take a look as people build Leonardo's self-supporting bridge today!

Kids See This Leonardo bridge

Leonardo made another important innovation while working for Borgia. Using his skills with art and observation, he drew an accurate, **aerial**-view map of the town of Imola. An aerial-view map shows a town from above. Today, we see maps like this all the time, but back then, before airplanes, satellites, and drones had been invented, this was highly unusual.

Having an accurate map of a town would give military leaders an incredible advantage. They could plan attacks and look for weak spots.

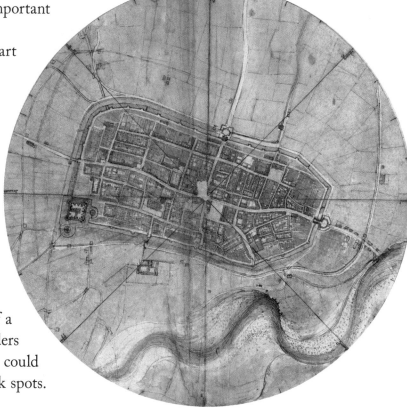

Leonardo's aerial map of Imola

Leonardo also indicated accurate distances on this map. Leonardo built and used an odometer, a device that can measure distance. The odometer was a little cart on wheels. Every time the wheels made a full **revolution**, a second, horizontal wheel moved one notch. When the horizontal wheel moved a notch, a stone fell into a container. If the odometer moved one foot with each revolution, Leonardo could count the stones and know the distance he had traveled.

What do people use to MEASURE DISTANCE today?

Take a look at this modern version of the pulley system designed by Leonardo.

Da Vinci Bruges exhibition

PS

Make Art Not War

Not all of Leonardo's engineering designs were for war. When he moved to Milan, he recorded in his notebook some ideas for his ideal artist's studio. He thought of adjustable blinds to control how much light came in through the windows. He also described a system of pulleys and platforms that would raise and lower easels. Moving the painting would be much more convenient than the painter climbing ladders or squatting on the floor. Think of your own bedroom or kitchen. How could you improve the design so the room functions better?

MACHINE POWER

Leonardo didn't design machines just for fun—he liked to design machines that were useful. His goal was to create machines that solved problems and did useful tasks.

Machines need power to operate. Since batteries and electrical power weren't available in the Renaissance, the source of power for machines was people. People turned cranks or walked on treadmills to make machines move or work.

WORDS TO KNOW

perpetual: never stopping.

physics: the study of physical forces, including matter, energy, and motion, and how these forces interact with each other.

simple machine: a device with few or no moving parts. It performs work by changing motion and force. There are six main kinds: inclined **plane**, lever, wedge, wheel and axle, pulley, and screw.

plane: a flat surface.

Archimedes' screw: a simple machine used to pump water uphill. A screw is inside a cylinder or tube. The bottom goes into the water. A handle turns the screw and carries the water up a slope.

Because people were the source of his power, Leonardo wanted to know exactly how the human body worked. How much force could arm muscles deliver? How strong were leg muscles? Which muscles were stronger? As usual for Leonardo, his work in one field—engineering—was connected to his studies in another field—human anatomy. If he understood the human body perfectly, he could better design machines that would work using human power.

Water was another source of power for machines, both then and now. Leonardo loved studying water. He loved painting it and designing machines that used the flow of water to function.

Leonardo hoped to use the power of falling water to create a **perpetual** motion machine. A perpetual motion machine is one that keeps moving or operating under its own power. It doesn't slow down and doesn't need an outside power source. Leonardo was exploring ideas in **physics** that would take another 200 years to be understood by another innovator, Isaac Newton (1643–1727).

We still use hydropower today, just as this dam is doing.

Welcome to Milan

One of Leonardo's engineering projects was a redesign of the city of Milan. He wanted the city split into two layers. The top would be clean and beautiful while the lower level would handle sewage and garbage. In his new, beautiful city, he drew only spiral staircases. He didn't like corners, because men often relieved themselves in corners—Leonardo hated this! He also added public toilets to his redesign of Milan. These public bathrooms had lots of air vents and even swiveling toilet seats. How would you redesign your town to make it cleaner and more functional?

Could water be used to create a perpetual motion machine? Leonardo filled 28 pages of a notebook exploring and experimenting with his idea for this machine. He considered using a **simple machine** called an **Archimedes' screw**. As water was carried up one screw, it would also flow down another. Could the force of water flowing down keep the machine running forever? Leonardo decided it could not. So far, he has not been proven wrong.

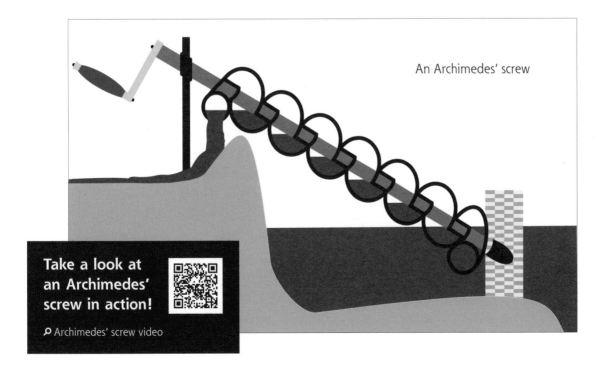

An Archimedes' screw

Take a look at an Archimedes' screw in action!

🔎 Archimedes' screw video

WORDS TO KNOW

resistance: a force that slows down another force.

eliminate: to get rid of.

slope: a surface that has one end higher than the other end.

displace: to replace fluid with an object. The weight of the water that is moved is equal to the weight of the object.

automaton: a moving mechanical device that imitates a human.

One of the reasons a perpetual motion machine doesn't work is because of friction. Friction is when one substance rubs against another. Friction slows things down and costs energy. Friction causes **resistance**, such as water resistance and air resistance.

If he was ever going to create a perpetual motion machine, Leonardo would have to find a way to **eliminate** friction. He dove into experiments studying friction, including carefully observing objects moving down a **slope**. He learned about the three elements of friction: the smoothness or roughness of the surface, the steepness of the slope, and the weight of the object.

Eureka!

Archimedes (287 BCE–212 or 211 BCE) lived in ancient Greece centuries before Leonardo. He was a mathematician and inventor. He is most famous for solving a problem for King Hiero. The king wanted to know if a crown he'd had made was of pure gold. Archimedes found a way to figure that out when he noticed water spilling out of his bathtub as he got in. He shouted "Eureka!," or "I have found it!" He discovered he could put a piece of pure gold that was exactly the same size as the crown into water and measure how much water it **displaced**. If the crown displaced the same amount of water then it, too, was pure gold.

FRICTION would be **especially important** when Leonardo investigated FLYING MACHINES.

This last point was very important, because the old idea was that the size of the object was a factor in creating friction. But Leonardo realized that weight, rather than size, is important. This idea wouldn't be relearned for 200 years.

The First Robots—Or Not?

Historians believe Leonardo da Vinci built the first robots—500 years ago! Some historians say a more accurate term is an **automaton**, or a machine that moves without human help. When Leonardo went to live with King Francis I in 1516, he built three lions that moved on their own. Unfortunately, there is nothing in Leonardo's notebooks that describes how they worked. But historical records say the first person to create automatons was Ibn Ismail ibn al-Razzaz Jazari (1136–1206), an Arab Muslim scholar working more than 800 years ago! Jazari built automaton peacocks, a musical robot band, and a hand-washing automaton that had a flushing mechanism. Jazari's flush mechanism is the same mechanism used in modern flushing toilets.

Leonardo learned that adding oil helps increase the smoothness and reduce friction. He also thought of putting ball bearings into his machines to reduce friction. The balls would create a smoother motion. It's unknown if Leonardo ever built a perpetual motion machine.

We've mentioned that Leonardo was fascinated with human anatomy. In the next chapter, we'll see how he used his powers of observation and experimentation to learn more about the human body!

This model is based on Leonardo's drawing of a perpetual motion machine.

ESSENTIAL QUESTION

How does understanding the parts of a machine help you understand how the machine works?

MEASURE THE MILES:
BUILD AN ODOMETER

An odometer made it easier for Leonardo to measure distances and draw more accurate maps. Try making your own odometer and use it to measure distances around your home. Use your science journal as a place to keep track of your measurements.

❱ **Draw a small dash or line on the side of your cylinder.**

❱ **Wrap the string around your cylinder.** Start with one end of the string at the mark you made.

❱ **When the string goes all the way around the cylinder and meets the start, make a mark on your string.** Cut the string at the mark.

❱ **Measure the string along the ruler.** Record the measurement. This is the **circumference** of your cylinder.

❱ **Secure a paper clip on the opening of your cylinder.** Line it up with your mark. Make sure the paper clip extends a little beyond the edge of your cylinder.

❱ **Start your odometer with the paper clip on the floor.** Roll your odometer. Every time the paper clip touches the floor, that's one revolution. Each revolution covers the distance that is equal to the circumference of your cylinder.

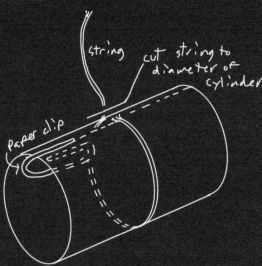

string

cut string to diameter of cylinder

paper clip

Think Like Leo!

Is this odometer as **precise** as a measuring tape? Compare your measurements with the two devices.

WORDS TO KNOW

circumference: the distance around a circle.

precise: exact, very accurate.

TEXT TO WORLD

Think of a device you use every day, such as an electric toothbrush or a bicycle. How could you improve on that invention to better suit your purposes?

LAUNCH TIME:
BUILD A CATAPULT

A catapult was a common piece of military equipment during the Renaissance. You can build one yourself and try some experiments with it. Think about how you would make it better.

❱ **Stack five popsicle sticks on top of one another.** Secure them tightly with a rubber band at each end. This is your base.

❱ **Take two more popsicle sticks and stack them on top of one another.** Secure them with a rubber band but only at one end. This is part of the catapult arm.

❱ **Slide the base in between the open end of the arm.**

❱ **Wrap a rubber band around BOTH the arm and the base.** The rubber band should make an X around the arm.

❱ **Glue the bottle cap to the part of the arm high in the air.**

❱ **Launch small projectiles, such as marshmallows or pompoms.**

Think Like Leo!

Try some experiments with your catapult. Make sure you record your observations in your science journal. Does your projectile go farther if you pull the arm back farther? Or does it go higher? How does the weight of the projectile change how high it flies? How does its weight change how far it flies?

Make a second catapult and glue a plastic spoon to the arm. This makes the arm longer. How does this change how far your projectile travels?

FRICTION STRUCTURE: BUILD A
SELF-SUPPORTING BRIDGE

INVENTOR KIT

° pieces of wood such as popsicle sticks or balsa wood for bridge sides

° wooden dowels for bridge steps

Leonardo designed a bridge that was strong enough to hold people but did not have posts in the water or wires holding it up. It relied only on friction and gravity to hold the wood pieces in place. The bridge is made by weaving pieces of wood over and under other pieces. It's complicated and takes practice. Build your bridge and test its strength. Take notes in your notebook and draw your finished bridge.

❯ **Lay out two side pieces side by side.** They should be closer together than the length of the step pieces.

❯ **Slide a step piece (S1) under the two side pieces.** It should be on the left side.

❯ **Lay another step piece (S2) over the two side pieces.** This one should be right in the middle.

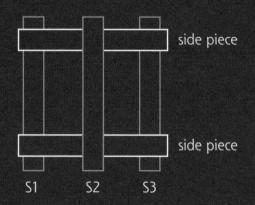

side piece

side piece

S1   S2   S3

❯ **Now, slide another step piece (S3) under the two side pieces.** This one should be on the right side.

❯ **Take two new side pieces.** Slide them under S3 and over S2 as shown, close together.

❯ **Slide a new step piece (S4) under the right edges of the new side pieces.**

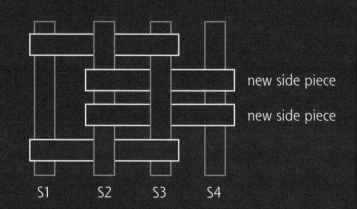

new side piece

new side piece

S1   S2   S3   S4

▶ **Take two new side pieces.** Lay them over S4 and under S3 as shown.

▶ **Lay a new step piece (S5) over the right ends of the new side pieces.**

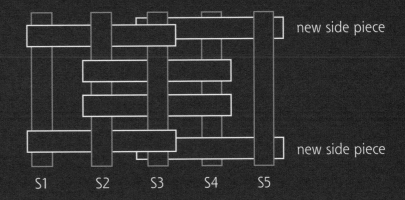

new side piece

new side piece

S1   S2   S3   S4   S5

▶ **Place two new side pieces over S5 and under S4.** Do you see how you're creating a woven pattern in your bridge?

▶ **Lay more sections in this pattern until you think your bridge is ready to stand on its own.** Does it work? Do you need to make adjustments? Can you make any improvements to the design?

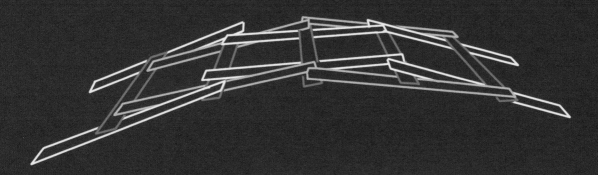

Think Like Leo!

Building materials matter. What building materials work best for this kind of bridge? How would making a bridge like this out of dry spaghetti pasta change the strength of the bridge? What are the pros and cons of using pieces of metal? What other materials might work that Leonardo didn't have?

CONDUCT
FRICTION EXPERIMENTS

Leonardo conducted many experiments to learn about friction. He wanted to figure out a way to reduce friction and create smooth movement in his machines. Do some of your own friction tests and record the results in your notebook.

❯ **Make a chart in your science notebook** of your surfaces and objects.

❯ **Set up your ramp.** Lean one edge of your sliding surface on a stair or on a stack of books.

❯ **Hold an object at the top of the ramp.** Get your timer ready.

❯ **When you push the object onto the ramp, start your stopwatch.** Time how long each object takes to move down the ramp. Record the times in your chart.

	Toy Car	Bean Bag
Whiteboard		
Cardboard box		
Corkboard		
Large book		
Smooth board		
Rough board		

❯ **Test each object with different surfaces.** Which object slides down all slopes fastest? Which slides down the slowest?

Think Like Leo!

The incline of your ramp is how steep (high) or flat (low) it is. If you change the incline by making it higher or lower, does that change the speed of objects? What if the slope is flat? If you make the toy car heavier, does that change its speed?

Leonardo decided that the weight of an object is more important than the size of an object in causing friction. Test two books of the same size but different weights, such as a textbook and a picture book. In your notebook, record their speeds. What do you observe?

Chapter 3

GETTING UNDER THE SKIN:
ANATOMY

Leonardo's studies of anatomy began, like much of his learning, in the studio of Verrocchio. As an apprentice, Leonardo needed to learn how to draw and paint people and animals.

Anatomy is the study of the structure of a body. This includes humans and animals. Anatomy is usually learned by dissecting a body and studying each part separately. It might sound disgusting, but dissection is a very useful learning tool that is still used today, and it means that bodies have a useful function even after death.

ESSENTIAL QUESTION

How did Leonardo apply what he learned about the human body to his other areas of study?

Leonardo used the same process to study humans that he used with machines. Remember, Leonardo drew machines in their separate parts to understand how they worked when they were fully assembled.

WORDS TO KNOW

organ: a part of an **organism** that has a specific job, such as the heart or stomach.

organism: something living, such as a plant or an animal.

spinal cord: a bundle of nerves in the spine that connects the body with the brain.

Take a look at some of Leonardo's anatomy drawings. What do they make you think of?

🔍 Nature video Leonardo

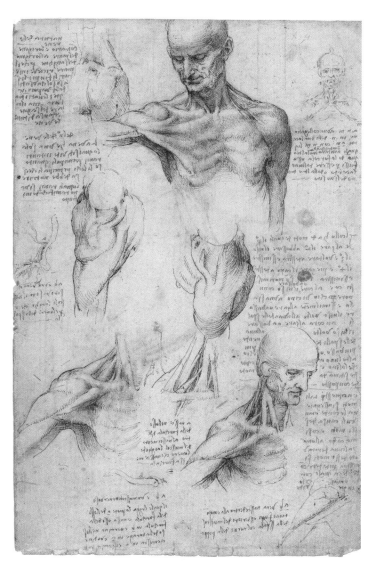

For human bodies, Leonardo studied the **organs**, muscles, and bones inside people. He sketched them as separate pieces so he could understand how they looked and worked. This meant that when he painted people, they looked real, because he knew how bodies were built. And, as usual, he recorded everything he learned in his notebooks.

Leonardo's art shows how well he understood the human body and the human mind. He wrote, "Movements should announce the motions of the mind."

DISSECTION

Lift your arm to your face. Point your toe out in front of you. How are you able to control your motions so well? What complex systems inside of you are working to accomplish these simple tasks?

When Leonardo drew or painted people, he wanted them to look as real as possible. To do that, he needed to learn how the muscles of the human body looked and worked. When he began to really understand muscles, he realized he needed to know how the nerves and the brain controlled the muscles. Dissection was the only way to gain this knowledge.

Leonardo said that looking at his drawings should feel **"EXACTLY as if you had that SAME LIMB in your hand** and were turning it from side to side."

When Leonardo moved to Milan in 1482, his study of anatomy became more intense. He wrote down all of the questions he had about the human body.

Find the Spine

Leonardo dissected animals as well as humans. During one investigation, he wanted to know what parts of the body were essential for life. He cut off a frog's head, internal organs, and skin. The frog still lived. But when he cut the **spinal cord**, the frog died. In this way, Leonardo learned how important the spinal cord was to keeping the frog alive. This experiment wouldn't be described by scientists again until the 1700s.

Do you think scientific discovery is worth cruelty to animals? Are there other ways to make this kind of discovery?

WORDS TO KNOW

invested: to be deeply involved and interested.

exterior: on the outside of something.

interior: on the inside of something.

methodical: using a system or following steps to do something.

veins: blood vessels without muscles in their walls that carry blood to the heart.

arteries: blood vessels with muscles in their walls that carry blood from the heart.

blood vessel: a thin tube in an animal's body that carries blood.

arteriosclerosis: the hardening of artery walls, especially in old age.

Some of these questions were simple. He wanted to know, "What nerve is the cause of closing the eyelid?"

Others were complex. He wanted to know what "nerve is the cause of laughing and expressing wonder." He also asked, "What yawning is" and what causes sleep, hunger, and sneezing.

When Leonardo set out to study something, he became fully **invested** in his subject. He decided he would draw parts of the human body from at least three different points of view. He wanted his drawings to be completely accurate.

Next to his **SKULL DRAWINGS**, Leonardo made notes about human teeth. He described the four types and wrote that adults typically have **32 teeth. This made him the** first person ever to describe **HUMAN DENTAL PARTS!**

He started his anatomical drawings around 1488. His first drawings were of skulls. He drew one skull in two halves. One half shows the **exterior**, one shows the **interior**. Leonardo used his mastery of art to show how the skull was curved in some places, hollow in others. Put the two halves together and they give a full picture of how the skull looks and functions.

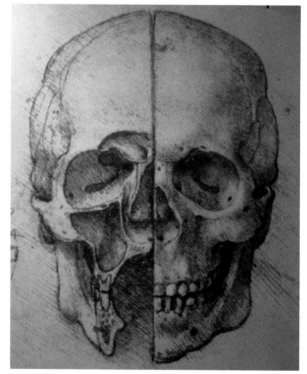

This skull drawing was mind-blowing. Previous artists hadn't drawn things like this before. This style of anatomical drawing is still used today.

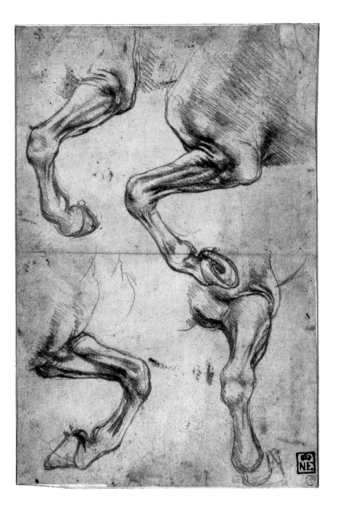

Leonardo did a lot of work dissecting and drawing human bodies from 1508 to 1513. He was very careful and **methodical**. He started by drawing the muscles covered with skin, then the muscles without skin, then **veins** and **arteries** and internal organs. He observed, drew, and took notes.

He observed the **blood vessels** of a very old man and noticed they were thick and blocked. The blood vessels of a young child were flexible and wide open. Leonardo was describing what we now call **arteriosclerosis**, or hardening of arteries.

Leonardo dissected about 20 bodies. This was not easy work! There was no way to preserve the bodies or prevent them from decomposing, since there was no refrigeration or chemicals.

Where to Find Feelings

When Leonardo diagrammed the skull, he marked its center. Was this place in the brain the source of human emotion? As he drew the skull, he theorized that all of the senses might meet in the center of the brain. This is where he thought the soul or source of emotions might be. He was looking for what he called the "senso comune," or the meeting of the senses. Where are some other places in the body that people have hypothesized feelings come from?

WORDS TO KNOW

tendon: flexible cords that attach muscles to bones.

ventricle: a hollow part of an organ.

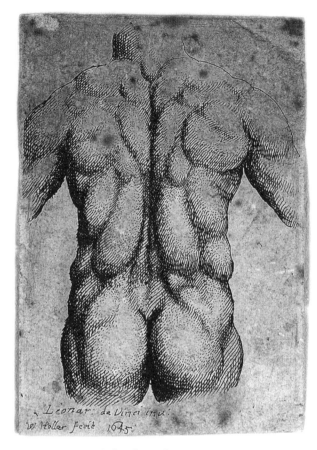

Credit: Wellcome Collection (CC By 4.0)

The smell alone would stop many people from this educational journey. And, if the smell wasn't bad enough, there was always the dark.

Dissection was allowed only at night in the hospital. Picture Leonardo alone in a dark room full of corpses, lit only by candles. This was his laboratory.

What are some of the ways Leonardo embodied CURIOSITY?

Leonardo could have attended a class on anatomy, where an instructor would lecture and an assistant would hold up parts of the body for students to see, from a distance. But there, the instructor would tell the students what to write down, what to look at, what others had discovered.

How dissections were usually done in the past

Credit: Christopher Wright, 1665, Wellcome Collection (CC By 4.0)

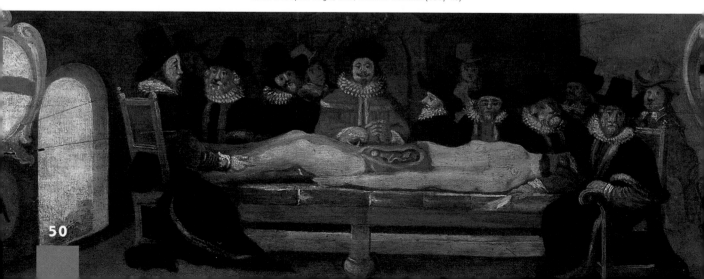

That was never Leonardo's style. He was always committed to observing and learning for himself.

Leonardo's experience with engineering helped him understand how muscles, bones, **tendons**, and nerves work together. "The joints between bones obey the tendon, and the tendon obeys the muscle, and the muscle the nerve," he wrote.

As Leonardo studied the **HUMAN JAW**, he decided to learn about a **CROCODILE'S JAW.** Crocodile jaws have a second joint. Their bite is **30 TIMES STRONGER** than a human bite!

He saw the human body as a collection of simple machines. He noted that muscles connect two bones together. They don't start and end on the same bone—if they did, nothing could move. This seems logical now, but had anyone before Leonardo explained this?

Leonardo applied his experience as a sculptor to understanding the human brain. Using a cow's brain, he injected wax into the spaces inside, called **ventricles**. When the wax cooled, he pulled the brain apart and had a perfect mold of the inside spaces of the brain.

Tongues and Jaws

Leonardo loved making connections between humans and nature. As he learned about the human tongue, he made a note to himself to learn about a woodpecker's tongue. Tongues are unique muscles. Most muscles act by pulling on joints, but tongues push on joints. And woodpecker's tongues are even more unique. They are long enough to wrap around their skulls and cushion their brains during the force of pecking.

 PS Take a look at this video showing how a hummingbird uses its tongue to drink.

🔎 NYT hummingbird tongue

WORDS TO KNOW

emotion: a strong feeling about something or someone.

circulatory system: the body system that carries blood and other **fluids** around the human body. It includes the heart, blood, and blood vessels.

fluid: a substance that can flow and take the shape of its container.

membrane: a thin layer or boundary in an organ or living thing.

valve: a device that controls the flow of liquid through a pipe or tube.

aorta: the main artery in the body.

THE HUMAN HEART

One thing Leonardo paid close attention to was the human heart. This was another area where he needed to use his knowledge of engineering, the behavior of liquid, human anatomy, and art—many different streams of knowledge contributed to his understanding of one thing.

At this time, many ideas about the heart were 12 centuries old. People thought blood was made in the liver and that the heart created something called "vital spirits." People also didn't realize that blood circulated around the body. They thought it was simply pushed back and forth.

This was a groundbreaking technique. No one had done this before! But Leonardo was simply using the same techniques he had learned working in Verrocchio's studio. He was applying what he learned in one field of study to others.

Smile!

Leonardo was dedicated to understanding how **emotions** and muscles were connected. He wrote that "the muscles which move the lips are more numerous in man [sic] than in any other animal." How did our emotions control our nerves, which then moved our muscles? Understanding these tiny, but numerous, muscles was essential to creating *Mona Lisa*'s mysterious smile.

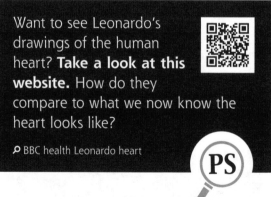

Want to see Leonardo's drawings of the human heart? **Take a look at this website.** How do they compare to what we now know the heart looks like?

🔎 BBC health Leonardo heart

PS

Leonardo made his own observations. And he realized these ideas were wrong. He learned that the heart was part of the **circulatory system**, which includes veins and arteries. He compared the circulatory system to a tree, rooted in the seed of the heart. Plus, he proved the heart was a muscle and showed the heart has four chambers, now called ventricles.

Each chamber in the heart was divided by a **membrane**. But the membranes weren't closed off. They had **valves** that allowed blood to flow through them as the heart pumped. But the most important discovery made by Leonardo was about how blood flows from the heart into the **aorta**, a large artery that carries blood from the heart to the rest of the body. There is a valve that opens and closes as blood flows from the heart into the aorta—but how?

The tricky thing about the aortic valve is that when it's open, the flaps of the valve are wrinkled and folded up. To close the valve, the flaps need to flatten and spread out. How did the flaps of the valve spread flat?

Leonardo understood how liquid flowed, and he understood friction. He knew that when water flowed through a pipe, the water that flowed against the sides of the pipe slowed down because of friction. The water in the center of the flow moved fastest.

WORDS TO KNOW

retina: the part of the eye containing light-sensitive cells that send electrical signals to the visual area of the brain for processing.

sternocleidomastoid: a muscle that is connected to the chest bone and clavicle and attaches to the skull. It bends, rotates, and flexes the head.

People didn't change their thinking about how the AORTIC VALVE worked until the 1960s!

Leonardo used what he knew about water flowing through pipes to figure out how blood moved through the body. He described the heart pumping blood into the aorta. The blood in the center shoots forward fast. The sides of the flowing blood move more slowly.

The blood flowing on the sides hits the flaps and forms spirals. The spiraling blood flows into the wrinkled flaps. It fills and spreads out the edges of the valves. The flaps open, cover the valve, and close so blood doesn't go back into the heart.

Leonardo never published his studies, so people didn't learn about his idea. Instead, people theorized that blood filled the aorta all at the same rate until enough blood pushed back on the valve to close it.

Back in the 1500s, Leonardo already knew this wouldn't work. If blood just pushed on the flaps while they were wrinkled and crumpled, the flaps would not close the valve. He even made a model of a heart out of glass to prove his theory. He used water to model the flow of blood and put grass seeds in the water to make it easier to see the action of the flowing liquid.

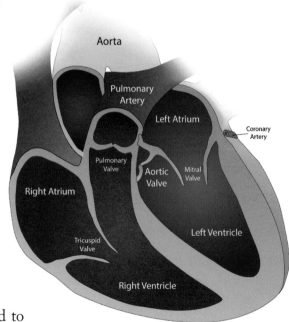

EYES

Leonardo loved studying eyes and vision. He wanted to paint them perfectly—he also wanted to understand how eyes worked and how viewers saw paintings.

At the time, most people thought human eyes collected light at one single point. But Leonardo questioned this. He had a theory that the entire back of the eye, called the **retina**, collected light. He decided to test his theory.

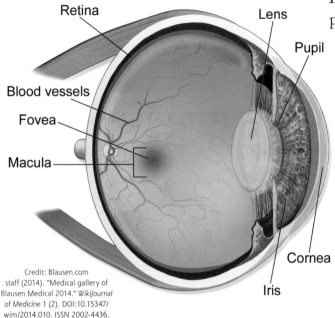

Retina

Lens

Pupil

Blood vessels

Fovea

Macula

Cornea

Iris

Credit: Blausen.com staff (2014). "Medical gallery of Blausen Medical 2014." *WikiJournal of Medicine* 1 (2). DOI:10.15347/wjm/2014.010. ISSN 2002-4436.

If eyes collected light on only one point, it should be possible to block that point with something very thin, such as a needle. He discovered that as the needle moved closer to the eye, it blocked a portion of vision, but not all vision. This proved to him that the entire retina collects light and images.

He knew that we do not see **SHARP OUTLINES** of things in nature and developed his **sfumato method to paint things and people as** realistically as possible.

FIXING MISTAKES

There is a secret clue in Leonardo's drawing of Saint Jerome that shows us how much his study of anatomy influenced his art. In the drawing, a holy man named Jerome kneels on the ground. It's obvious that he feels intense emotion, and his neck muscles are visible, including a major neck muscle called the **sternocleidomastoid**. This is actually a pair of muscles.

Hot-Blooded

Leonardo didn't know how blood was heated. He had a theory that the friction produced from the blood moving against the heart walls generated heat. He decided to test his theory by measuring the temperature of milk as it was churned into butter. Test this theory yourself by shaking milk in a small container and recording the results. Was Leonardo right?

WORDS TO KNOW

pupil: the dark opening in the center of the eye.

dilate: to become wider, more open.

contract: to shrink or make smaller.

anisocoria: a condition in which the pupils in someone's eyes are different sizes.

But in 1480, when Leonardo drew this, he didn't know it was a pair of muscles. In some drawings from 1495, he shows this part of the body as only one muscle. He did not learn it was two muscles until he explored this region of the human body via dissection in 1510.

How did he get it right in a drawing from 1480?

Most Renaissance portraits showed women from the **SIDE VIEW ONLY**. Leonardo painted some women in profile, but his later works show them in a **THREE-QUARTER VIEW**. This meant the viewer could see both eyes of the woman, which encouraged the perception of the figure as a **REAL PERSON**.

A Mistake in the *Mona Lisa*?

Leonardo knew that the **pupils** of the eye **dilate** to allow in more light when the environment is dim or dark. The pupils **contract** in bright light. In the *Mona Lisa*, her right pupil is larger than her left. But her right eye is closer to the light source. It should be smaller. Was this a simple mistake? Leonardo understood light and optics and the workings of the eye very well. Was it on purpose? Some historians think the woman in the painting had **anisocoria**, a condition in which one pupil is always larger than the other. Other historians think Leonardo knew human pupils dilate when a person is happy. Did Leonardo want viewers to think *Mona Lisa* was smiling just for them? It's another historical mystery.

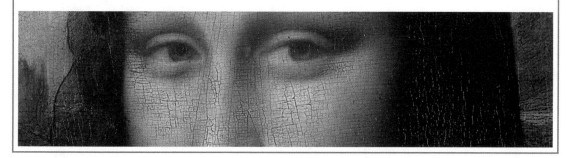

The answer lies in Leonardo's process. He never felt a painting or drawing was completely done. He'd return to the work over and over, for years and years, perfecting it slowly as time passed and he gained more knowledge.

His first drawings of Saint Jerome contained a mistake. When he learned the right way to draw the muscle, he went back and fixed it, 30 years later.

Art, engineering, anatomy—what else did Leonardo study? Something that ties all of these subjects together—mathematics! We'll learn more in the next chapter.

ESSENTIAL QUESTION

How did Leonardo apply what he learned about the human body to his other areas of study?

PUMP IT: BUILD A
HEART MODEL

Leonardo knew the heart was a muscle that pumped blood. Make your own model to observe how the heart pumps blood through our circulatory system.

❯ **Fill the jar half full of water.** If you're using red food coloring, add a few drops.

❯ **Cut off the neck of the balloon where it widens.** Set the neck part aside.

❯ **Stretch the balloon over the opening of the jar.** Pull it down tight. If it won't stay, you can use rubber bands to hold it in place.

❯ **Carefully poke two small holes, about 1 inch apart, in the surface of the balloon.** They should be near opposite edges of the jar. Keep the holes small.

❯ **Stick the long part of a straw into each hole.** The straws should fit tightly in the holes so no air can get in around the straws.

❯ **Slide the uncut end of the neck of the balloon on to one straw.** Tape it to the straw. This represents the valve.

❯ **Put your "heart" into the sink to catch the pumped water.** Bend the straws downward.

❯ **Gently press in the center of the stretched balloon.** What happens to the water in the jar?

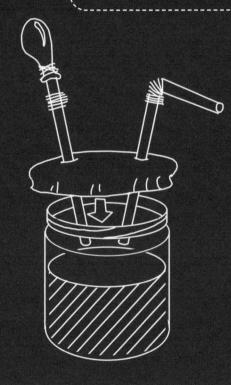

INVENTOR KIT

° beaker or wide-mouth jar
° water
° red food coloring (optional)
° large balloon
° rubber bands if needed
° 2 bending drinking straws
° large pan or sink

Think Like Leo!

Take the valve off of the straw and pump the heart model. How does it work differently this time?

TEXT TO **WORLD**

Do you play sports, dance, or ride a bike? How does knowing how your muscles work help you with anything physical?

CREATE A
SPINE

INVENTOR KIT
° egg carton
° felt
° chenille stems

Leonardo drew a detailed diagram of the human spine. He drew the spine completely assembled, and, in his signature style, drew close-ups of each individual **vertebra**. The human spine has 33 bones. You can make a small model, or if you have enough supplies, make the full spine.

❯ **Cut the egg carton apart so each cup is separate.**

❯ **Cut out felt circles.** The circles should be a little smaller than the egg cups. Cut one fewer than the number of egg cups you plan to use.

❯ **Using a pencil, or the point of the scissors, carefully punch a hole in the sides of each egg cup.** The holes should be opposite one another.

❯ **Thread a chenille stem through each hole of the first egg cup.**

❯ **Add one felt circle above the egg cup.** This felt circle represents the disc that cushions each vertebra.

❯ **Add another egg cup and another felt disk to the chenille stem.** When you run out of room, twist another chenille stem onto the first to make a longer stem.

❯ **Add more egg cups and felt circles until your spine is complete.**

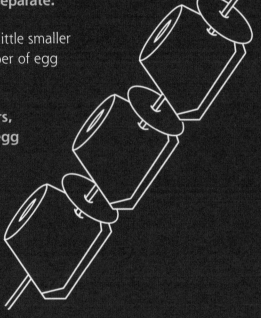

Think Like Leo!

What if you removed the felt circles and moved the spine model a lot? How would that affect the "vertebrae" (egg cartons)? What if you used a pencil instead of a chenille stem? How would that change how the spine model moved?

WORDS TO KNOW

vertebra: one of the small bones that form the backbone. Plural is vertebrae.

MODEL A
HUMAN JOINT

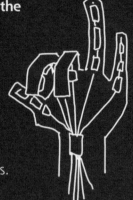

A joint is a place where bones meet. There are different kinds of joints in the human body—try building a hinge joint in this activity.

❯ **Trace and cut out the outline of your hand onto the cardboard.** Tape a piece of string to each fingertip.

❯ **Thread the string through the pasta tubes.** The string should come down as long as the wrist. Tape the pasta tubes to the fingers. Try to put them where the bones in your fingers are. Leave some room between them for joints.

❯ **The string represents your muscles.** As you pull on the string, this simulates a nerve contracting a muscle in the finger. Muscles pull on bones and bend the joints.

Think Like Leo!

Look at how your fingers bend. Do they bend at every joint? Can you control each joint in one finger independently? What other hinge joints are in your body? How do thumbs move differently than fingers? The thumb connects to the hand in a saddle joint. What does this tell you about saddle joints compared to hinge joints?

Types of Joints

There are six kinds of joints in the human body—hinge, ball-and-socket, pivot, saddle, gliding, and condyloid. The bones in the neck are pivot joints. The hip is a ball-and-socket joint. Small bones in the hand and wrist are gliding joints and condyloid joints.

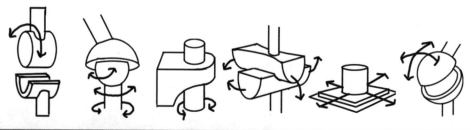

WATER AS A
LENS

INVENTOR KIT
- ° paper
- ° marker
- ° clear glass
- ° pitcher or bottle of water

Leonardo understood that the lens in our eyes is **convex**. This means that the image that is sent to our brain is upside down. He didn't know that our brain was able to flip the image right-side up. Try this simple experiment with another convex lens.

❯ **Draw an arrow pointing to the right on the middle of your paper and stand your paper up.** You can secure your paper to a wall or a stack of books or a cereal box.

❯ **Line up the glass in front of the paper.** Place it so you can see the arrow through the glass.

❯ **Pour the water into the glass.** As you pour, observe the arrow. Where is it pointing now?

❯ **Move the glass out of the way.** The arrow is still pointing right. But the water acts as a convex lens and flips the image the other way around.

Think Like Leo!

What happens to the image of the arrow when you use two glasses? Does it point in the original direction? Why or why not?

Learning from Alhazen

Leonardo wasn't the first person to study vision. Ibn al-Haytham (965–1040), known as Alhazen, was a **physicist** born in the region we now call Iraq. He performed experiments, made observations, and developed theories about human vision—400 years before Leonardo da Vinci. Alhazen's method of exploring a subject influenced how Leonardo worked.

Watch a short movie about Alhazen and his scientific pursuits.

🔎 1001 inventions Haytham

WORDS TO KNOW

convex: a rounded shape like the outside of a bowl.

physicist: a scientist who studies physical forces, including matter, energy, and motion, and how these forces interact with each other.

Chapter 4

VISUALIZING NUMBERS:
MATHEMATICS

WHAT IS THIS?

IT'S AN ABACUS.

ISN'T THAT FOR FIGURING OUT MATH PROBLEMS? I THOUGHT YOU MADE ART?

It might seem as though math and art exist at opposite ends of the creativity spectrum, but actually the two disciplines support each other. Art is very mathematical, and math is very creative. Leonardo understood this fundamentally.

As an apprentice, Leonardo learned math on an **abacus**, a device used for counting and calculations. In the past, the abacus was used around the world, from China and Russia to Europe. An abacus has a frame with rods. On each rod are a certain number of counters—often these counters look like beads. People would slide the counters up and down the rods to count and do **arithmetic**, including addition, subtraction, multiplication, and division.

ESSENTIAL QUESTION

How did Leonardo's artistic skills help him with mathematics?

As an apprentice to Verrocchio, who was a craftsman artist, the young Leonardo needed to know how to keep track of his expenses and his income. An abacus helped him with that. He learned to use the abacus for practical situations, such as paying for supplies and charging for artwork.

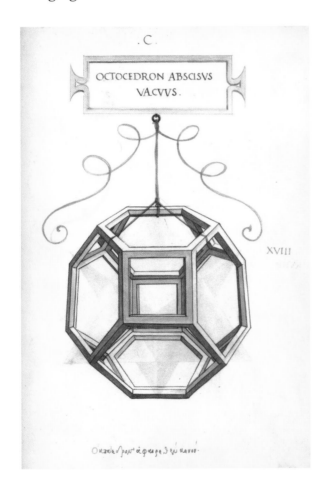

Most artists did not dive into the deeper studies of math.

But Leonardo da Vinci wasn't most artists.

GEOMETRY

Leonardo first studied geometry during his time as an apprentice with Verrocchio. Drawing accurate, lovely geometric shapes was a part of his work as an artist.

Geometry seemed to come naturally to Leonardo—he loved the artistic side of math, especially drawing three-dimensional (3-D) shapes. Leonardo probably did some of his first geometric artwork on a tomb, a project in Verrocchio's studio that featured carvings of a circle inside a square.

WORDS TO KNOW

Platonic shapes: a set of five shapes, all of which have faces that are regular **polygons** of the same size and all the vertices (corners) are identical. Also known as Platonic slides.

polygon: a geometric figure with at least three straight sides and angles.

polyhedron: a solid in three dimensions with flat polygonal faces, straight edges, and sharp vertices.

vertex: a meeting point where two lines form an angle. Plural is vertices.

golden ratio: when two numbers have a ratio that is the same as the ratio of their sum to the larger of the two quantities.

ratio: the comparison of two numbers to each other.

proportion: the balanced relationships between parts of a whole.

algebra: using letters and symbols to represent numbers and amounts in equations and formulas.

In his time working for the duke of Milan, Leonardo became friends with a famous mathematician named Luca Pacioli (1447–1517), who tried to help Leonardo improve his math skills. Leonardo thanked Pacioli by drawing incredibly realistic geometric shapes for Pacioli's book, *On Divine Proportion*. This book described the five **Platonic shapes**. Platonic shapes were named after the Greek philosopher Plato (c. 423–c. 347 BCE), but humans had known about these shapes for centuries.

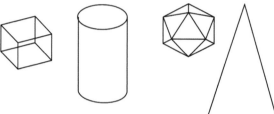

The five Platonic shapes are **polyhedrons**. Polyhedrons are three-dimensional solids that have the same number of sides meeting at each corner, or **vertex**. The shapes Leonardo drew were pyramids, cubes, octahedrons, dodecahedrons, and icosahedrons. He even drew a rhombicuboctahedron—this shape has 26 faces!

These geometric shapes had been drawn before. But Leonardo loved to innovate. He used his artistic brilliance to draw them in a new way.

He drew each shape in a way that made them look transparent and used his knowledge of light and shadow to give each shape a three-dimensional quality. The edges look like beams. Leonardo could probably visualize each shape in his head, but it's also likely he had a model of each shape made out of wood. Leonardo drew 60 of these illustrations for Pacioli.

These 60 shapes are the only drawings Leonardo ever published in his lifetime. Leonardo made **HUNDREDS OF DRAWINGS** and wrote **THOUSANDS OF PAGES,** but he never published most of them. Other people published his drawings and writings after he died.

The Golden Ratio

Pacioli's book, *On Divine Proportion*, explored an idea called the **golden ratio,** or "divine proportion." A **ratio** is a comparison of two numbers. For example, consider the number of raisins compared to chocolate chips in an oatmeal raisin chocolate chip cookie. If there are twice as many raisins, the ratio is 2:1.

The golden ratio is the idea that you can divide a line into two unequal parts at a place where the ratio between the whole and the longer part is equal to the ratio between the longer and shorter part. The golden ratio is important because it showed a system that was always in perfect **proportion** to itself.

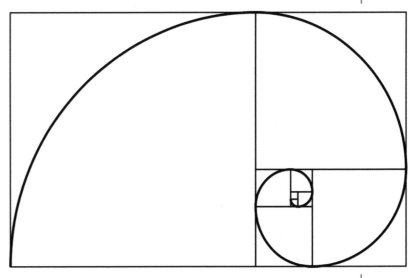

This golden spiral illustrates the golden ratio.

Leonardo would have had trouble doing the **algebra** for the golden ratio, but he would have been able to draw it perfectly.

WORDS TO KNOW

conservation of volume: the concept that a substance, such as a liquid, stays the same quantity even if its appearance or shape changes.

volume: the amount of space an object takes up or the amount of space inside an object.

VITRUVIAN MAN

When Leonardo was an apprentice, one of his first geometric design projects was for a tomb. The tomb had a design of a circle drawn perfectly inside of a square. Leonardo explored this same design in one of the most famous challenges of his time: the *Vitruvian Man*.

Conservation of Volume

Leonardo mastered the art of drawing shapes in three-dimensional ways. He also loved studying the flow and properties of water. Combining these two skills helped him explore the idea of **conservation of volume**. Conservation of volume means that when you have an amount of water, even if its shape changes, the amount stays the same. Leonardo drew this concept out over and over again. He started with a sphere and changed it into a cube. Even though the shape changed, the **volume**—the amount of space inside each object—stayed the same.

VITRUVIUS WROTE,

"The distance from his chin to the top of his forehead should be one-tenth his whole height."

Vitruvian Man is the name of a drawing by Leonardo that combines his love of art, anatomy, and mathematics.

Vitruvius (c. 80–70 BCE–c. 15 BC) was an ancient Roman architect. He wrote that temples should be designed based on the proportions of the human body.

Vitruvius recorded many measurements and proportions of parts of the body. He believed that knowing the proportions of the body would help artists understand the proportions of things in nature, better enabling them to create works of true beauty. Leonardo read Vitruvius's work and agreed with him passionately.

Vitruvius inspired artists such as Leonardo to tackle a challenge: He described a man in a circle and a square. The man's navel, or belly button, should be the exact center of the circle and the square.

But no one had yet drawn this idea when, around 1490, Leonardo and his friends gave it a try. Several people participated and created wonderful drawings, but it was Leonardo who claimed the prize. He drew the same man in two positions, perfectly placed inside the geometric shapes of both a circle and a square.

Some historians think *Vitruvian Man* **is a** **SELF-PORTRAIT** of Leonardo da Vinci at age 38.

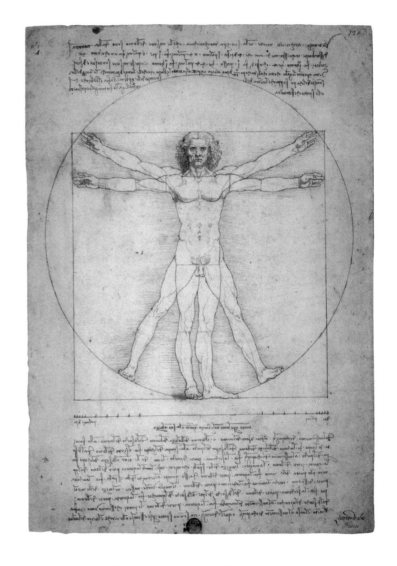

Leonardo could have used Vitruvius's measurements of the body to draw his *Vitruvian Man*. But, just as he handled all questions and challenges, he learned from his own observations. Using human models, he measured the proportions of human bodies—and then, he asked his models to move. He understood that bodies weren't statues and had to be considered as creatures in motion. Leonardo's models twisted, crouched, laid down, and he measured how proportions changed.

WORDS TO KNOW

hypotenuse: the longest side of a right triangle, opposite the right angle.

pi: the number represented by the symbol π and often shortened to 3.14.

THE ALTAR OF APOLLO

Leonardo struggled with another aspect of math: algebra. Algebra uses letters and symbols to represent numbers and amounts in equations and formulas. Instead of formulas, Leonardo used his artistic skills to help him visualize math problems in ways that made sense to him.

For example, he used art to tackle an ancient Greek riddle about the altar of Apollo, one of their gods. As the riddle goes, citizens in a Greek city experienced a plague. To stop the plague, they were told to double the size of an altar to Apollo, which was a cube. The problem was, if they doubled the sides, they ended up making a cube that was eight times bigger, not two times bigger! The ancient Greeks didn't have the mathematical skills to solve this problem. Neither did Leonardo.

But he did have the artistic skills.

Take a look at what made the *Vitruvian Man* so important in this video. Can you think of a piece of art that symbolized another time period as well as this one symbolized the Renaissance?

🔎 Ted Ed *Vitruvian Man* math

PS

Draw Objects in Three Dimensions

Leonardo drew incredible shapes and made them look real. He used shading and lines to create three-dimensional images. Here's how to draw a 3-D cube. Try it yourself! Draw a square on a page in your notebook. Now, draw four diagonal lines extending off the corners of square to the right. Now, draw a second square connecting those four lines. What happens if you shade two sides of the square? What happens if you shade the top and bottom? Can you draw the beams of the cube like Leonardo did for Pacioli?

Leonardo solved this problem by drawing a cube. Then, he drew a plane that cut the first cube in half diagonally. He drew a cube on that diagonal line. In mathematical terms, Leonardo squared the **hypotenuse** with these actions. But he didn't know that at the time, because he never really learned to master square roots, which was what he was doing in mathematical terms.

Leonardo **OFTEN MADE MISTAKES**. In one of his notebooks, he tried to calculate **4,096 + 4,096. His answer was 8,092. Was he** correct? No. The correct answer is 8,192. He made a simple mistake and **FORGOT TO CARRY THE ONE**.

Have Some Pi!

For more than 15 years, Leonardo tackled the puzzle of squaring a circle. This meant drawing a circle and a square with the same area using only a compass and a ruler. We now know this problem can't be solved by drawing. Mathematicians use a number called **pi**. Leonardo didn't know about this number. He never solved the problem, but the art he created while trying is visually incredible.

WORDS TO KNOW

dimension: when an object looks like it has length, width, and depth.

vanishing point: the point at which something grows smaller and smaller and almost disappears completely.

linear perspective: a way of drawing so that some things look closer to the viewer and some look farther away.

acuity: sharp, clear vision.

Leonardo explored mathematical concepts because he loved experimenting and tackling puzzles. At one point in 1501, his friend wrote, "His mathematical experiments have absorbed his thoughts so entirely that he cannot bear the sight of a paintbrush."

But understanding math also made Leonardo a better painter.

PERSPECTIVE IN ART

Leonardo's strong geometry skills improved his art to a great extent. Understanding how to draw shapes that look like they have depth and **dimension** would help Leonardo create paintings that looked incredibly real.

This is because Leonardo mastered the art of perspective. Perspective is a way of drawing that creates an illusion of space and depth. Using perspective can make flat images drawn on paper look rounded and real.

Leonardo wrote, "Perspective is the **BEST GUIDE** to the art of painting."

In order to draw with perspective, an artist needs to know about the **vanishing point** and the horizon. In art, the horizon is an imaginary line where the sky meets the ground. The vanishing point is a spot on the horizon where imaginary lines all come together.

Can you spot the vanishing point? How about the horizon?

Knowing and using the vanishing point helps art, especially landscapes and portraits, appear more real. Early in his career, Leonardo drew careful grid lines in order to get the perspective completely correct. While Leonardo didn't come up with the idea of **linear perspective**, he certainly mastered it.

In art, linear perspective means objects twice as far away appear half as big. Leonardo didn't have a calculator to help him practice this concept— he had to observe it and experiment with drawing it.

Leonardo also worked with another type of perspective— **acuity** perspective. Acuity is how clear something is. Leonardo wrote in his notebooks that things that were far away were less sharp and clear.

How does Leonardo use perspective in this painting, done between 1483 and 1486, called *The Virgin of the Rock*?

WORDS TO KNOW

atmosphere: the layer of gases surrounding a planet.

water vapor: the gas form of water in the air.

larynx: an organ in the throat that holds the vocal chords. Also called the voice box.

vibrate: to move back and forth or side to side very quickly.

pitch: how high or low a sound is, depending on its frequency.

improvise: inventing or creating something while you're doing it.

lyre: a stringed instrument, like a u-shaped harp.

viola organista: a musical instrument invented by Leonardo da Vinci. By pressing on keys, a moving belt made certain strings vibrate and produce sound.

He painted things in the distance this way, with fuzzy outlines and shapes. Objects in the distance also lose their true color and turn bluish-gray.

Leonardo's knowledge that things in the distance are blurry and their colors change shows how carefully he observed the world. He focused on every tiny detail as he explored many subjects. His understanding of why things look different in the distance hints that he understood about the **atmosphere**, a layer of air and **water vapor** surrounding the earth.

MATH IN MUSIC

When he joined the court of the duke of Milan, Leonardo was often asked to play and sing—he was famous for his ability to sing and play musical instruments. Interestingly, music is very mathematical. Leonardo understood that certain patterns and proportion in music create songs people like.

Connecting Anatomy to Music

Leonardo connected his studies of music to his understanding of human anatomy. He knew that there were vocal cords inside the human **larynx**. The larynx is located in the throat and is also called the voice box. He knew the vocal cords **vibrated** to make sounds and that if the vocal cords vibrated faster, the sound would have a higher **pitch**. If the cords vibrated slower, the pitch would be lower.

Even though Leonardo wrote so many of his ideas down in his notebooks, he didn't record his music—his songs were most often **improvised**.

Leonardo also understood the science of how instruments make sounds. He knew that the length and thickness of strings changed the tone they created, while the thickness of metal in a bell changed the sound it made. Leonardo used his artistic imagination, his understanding of engineering, and his understanding of mathematical patterns to invent his own musical instruments.

He constructed a **lyre**, or type of harp. Leonardo loved using nature as his inspiration, and the frame of his lyre was shaped like a horse head. It had seven strings, two of which were plucked while five were played with a bow.

His most interesting musical invention is the **viola organista**, a cross between a violin and an organ. He drew many versions of this instrument.

Sketches for a viola organista

Leonardo is often called a **polymath**. This is a person with A LOT OF KNOWLEDGE about many different subjects—it doesn't actually describe someone who is good at math.

Using Art to Solve Math

Leonardo worked on some of the same math puzzles studied by Alhazen, the Muslim scholar working 400 years before Leonardo. Alhazen wanted to use math to solve a puzzle from 150 CE. Here's the problem: When light hits a concave mirror, it reflects off of it. Alhazen wanted to calculate where the reflected light would hit on another surface. Leonardo investigated this, too, but since he wasn't very good at solving calculations, he used art to draw a solution to this puzzle.

In the viola organista, the player pressed keys, which pushed violin strings against bow strings. Since the bow was moved mechanically, it could hold a sound for as long as the musician wanted. This instrument could also play **chords**. It was a unique instrument that combined the variety of tones created by a keyboard with the sound of a stringed instrument. It is a classic Leonardo idea.

Math provided a strong foundation for much of Leonardo's creative and scientific work. In the next chapter, we'll see what he studied when he looked up at the sky above him and turned his discerning eye toward the stars and planets.

ESSENTIAL QUESTION

How did Leonardo's artistic skills help him with mathematics?

DRAW THE
VANISHING POINT

Learning how to draw the vanishing point can turn art from a flat picture into a realistic drawing. Leonardo mastered this skill. It is also called one-point perspective.

❯ **Start with a large piece of blank paper in your notebook.** Draw a horizon line sideways across the middle of the paper. Use a ruler to keep the line straight.

❯ **Make a dot on the horizon.**

❯ **Now, lightly draw a large X so that the center of the X is on the dot.** Start your X from the corners of the paper. The center of the two bottom lines of the X is the road.

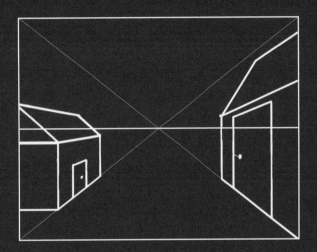

❯ **Now, draw objects to create your scene.** For this example, try drawing houses. The bases of the houses should sit on the bottom diagonal lines of the X. Remember, the objects close to the left and right edges of the paper are closest to the viewer, so these will be bigger. So, your houses close to the sides of the paper will be larger than the houses close to the dot at the center of the X.

❯ **Draw objects on both sides.**

❯ **The tops and bottoms of windows and doors should have diagonal lines that match the lines of your X.**

❯ **You can add more details as you practice drawing in one-point perspective.** Add color if you like! What does color add to the picture?

Think Like Leo!

Try drawing another picture with the horizon line higher and lower than the middle. How does this change how the viewer sees the picture? Try drawing another picture with the vanishing point off to the right or left. How does this change how the viewer sees the picture?

STRUM ON A
RUBBER BAND BOX LUTE

Leonardo loved to play music and sing. He was very popular in the court of the duke of Milan thanks to his musical skill. He also loved to invent instruments. Try making this simple rubber band box lute.

❯ **Stretch the five rubber bands around the box lengthwise.**

❯ **Play the lute by plucking the strings.** Listen to the tone of the sounds. What do they sound like?

❯ **Now, move the rubber bands.** Stretch them across the box sideways. How does changing the **tension** change the sound of the rubber bands?

❯ **Try stretching the rubber bands over a different material, such a coffee mug or a glass.** How does the material of the frame change the sound?

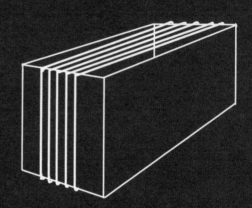

Think Like Leo!

Replace the rubber bands with other kinds of materials. Does string make the same kind of sound? What about tape?

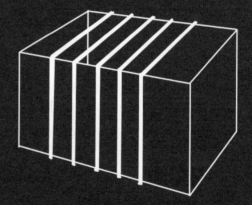

*TEXT TO **WORLD***
Where do you see connections between art and math? Literature and science?

WORDS TO KNOW

tension: a force that pulls or stretches an object.

STUDY
CONSERVATION OF VOLUME

INVENTOR KIT
° water
° containers of different sizes such as a square snack box, tall thin glass, short round glass, and large bowl

Leonardo knew an amount of water (or other liquid) stays the same even if you change the shape of the container it's in. Take a look.

❯ **Measure ½ cup of water and pour the water into one of the containers.**

❯ **Pour another ½ cup of water into a different container.** Does the amount of water in each container look different? Which one looks like it has more water? Why?

❯ **Ask a friend or classmate which container holds more.** Then, pour the water back into the measuring cup to prove it is the same amount.

Think Like Leo!

What other materials show conservation of volume? Can you show this concept with sugar? Salt? Beans?

The Wolf, the Goat, and the Cabbage

Leonardo loved the brain teasers that were described by his friend Pacioli. See if you can solve the following puzzle by drawing. A woman needs to carry a wolf, a goat, and a cabbage across the river. The rowboat can carry the woman and one other thing. The goat will eat the cabbage and the wolf will eat the goat, so those two can never be left alone together. How can the woman carry all three things across the river?

The solution: The wolf won't eat the cabbage, so the woman can take the goat first. She can row the boat back, then bring the cabbage over. Then, she leaves the cabbage and takes the goat back. She takes the wolf over and leaves it with the cabbage. She rows back alone and takes the goat back.

WATCH
SOUND TRAVEL

INVENTOR KIT

° box or flat board that is easy to hold from underneath

° rice, lentils, or flour (Leonardo used dust)

As he built musical instruments, Leonardo was still doing experiments. He didn't fully develop the idea of sound waves, but he had a basic understanding that sound traveled through air.

Leonardo performed experiments to learn about sound waves. He wrote that, "If you tap a board covered with dust, that dust will collect in diverse little hills."

❯ **Pour a small amount of your "dust" onto your board.** Tap the board from underneath.

❯ **Observe how the dust behaves.** Where does the dust settle? Is it close to where you are tapping? What shape do the little hills of dust form? How does the dust move as you tap?

❯ Leonardo wrote that, **"The hills will always pour down that dust from the tips of their pyramids to their base...[and] re-enter the underneath [rise up] through the center, and fall back again."** Do you find that to be true in your experiment?

Sound wave art can be pretty amazing. **Take a look at some of the designs that result from passing sound waves through different materials.**

🔎 sound wave video

PS

Think Like Leo!

How smooth is your board? If you use a board with a rough surface, does that change how the dust behaves? What concept does this show? (Hint: Look back at Chapter 2!)

LEONARDO'S
LUCKY 13

Here's a math trick from Leonardo. The answer always ends in 13. You can do this in your notebook or on a separate piece of paper.

❭ **Ask a friend to write down two columns.** Label them "Right Hand" and "Left Hand."

❭ **Have your friend pick a number.** Write down this number in both columns.

❭ **Tell your friend to subtract four from the right-hand column.** Add four to the left-hand column.

❭ **What is now in the right-hand column?** Your friend should subtract that from both the right-hand and the left-hand columns.

❭ **Your friend should now add five to the left-hand column.** Is the answer 13? Can you write an equation to show why that works?

Right Hand	Left Hand

Think Like Leo!

Leonardo might not have been great at algebra, but he was great at entertaining people with math tricks. Here's a simple one you can do with a friend and two sets of 12 items each. Have a friend pick a number less than 12. Ask them to count out that number of items. Remind them to keep this action hidden from you. Now, ask them to take enough items from you to add up to 12 when they add the two groups of items. You can now guess what number of items they had hidden.

MAKE YOUR OWN
ABACUS

Leonardo learned basic math at an abacus school. An abacus is a device for counting and calculating. Make one of your own.

❯ **String each chenille stem with 10 beads.** Evenly twist and wrap the ends of the chenille stems around the frame.

❯ **Each bead is a number.** Each row is a placeholder.

❯ **Practice counting.** Start by counting from one to 10 on the top row. Slide each bead from left to right.

❯ **When you want to count to 11, slide the first bead of the second row over from left to right.** Next, slide all of the beads in the top row back to the left. Now, move one bead in the top row to the right. This is 11.

❯ **Continue on to 19.** When you want to count to 20, slide two beads on the second row to the right and all of the beads in the top row back to the left.

Think Like Leo!

Count to eight by sliding eight beads from left to right on your top row.

Now, add seven by counting seven beads. Slide the beads over and count "one, two, ..." But you have only two beads left on your first row!

Slide one bead over to the right in your second row. This is the 10 bead.

Go back to the ones row. Slide all the beads to the left and keep counting as you move beads from left to right: "Three, four, five, six, seven."

You should have one bead in the tens row and five beads in the ones row on the right-hand side. Count all of the beads on the right. The answer to 8+7 is 15!

Chapter 5

ASTRONOMY &
LIGHT

Humans have observed the stars and planets for centuries. But ideas about how the planets move and what the solar system looks like haven't always been correct.

Before the Renaissance, most people believed the earth sat in the center of the solar system and the sun, planets, and stars moved around it. People used devices such as astrolabes to track the movement of planets. An astrolabe measures the **altitude** of things in space.

The movement of the planets supposedly influenced people's health. People studied where the planets were in the sky and believed they could use this information to predict the future. The position of certain planets in constellations could mean good fortune or terrible doom. This wasn't science—it was **astrology**.

ESSENTIAL QUESTION

How did Leonardo learn about space even though he could not leave Earth?

WORDS TO KNOW

solar system: the sun and eight planets that revolve around it.

altitude: the height of an object above sea level. Also called elevation.

astrology: the study of the movements of stars and planets and claiming they influence human actions and behaviors.

geocentric: a model of the universe, now disproved, that the earth is the center of the solar system.

orbit: the path of an object circling another in space.

heliocentric: a model of the universe in which the planets orbit the sun and the moon orbits the earth.

revolutionary: markedly new or introducing radical change.

Many incorrect ideas about astronomy were challenged during the Renaissance, thanks to Leonardo and other careful observers of the sky. During the Renaissance, people believed the planets and sun moved in perfect circles. Perfect circles were important—this meant that nature was in harmony and perfectly designed.

At the time Leonardo lived, most people believed in the **geocentric** model of the universe, which described the plants and sun **orbiting** around a stationary Earth, which was at the center of the solar system. This was the model that had always been supported by many famous scientists, including Plato and Aristotle.

During the Renaissance, a book by Greek scientist Ptolemy called *THE MATHEMATICAL COLLECTION* was considered the authority on the solar system. But most people knew the book by its Arabic title, *Almagest*. Arabic science was highly advanced and respected at this time.

The geocentric model of the solar system

Other scholars had argued that the earth and planets moved around the sun. This is called the **heliocentric** model. There is written evidence that the Indian philosopher Yajnavalkya, who lived in the 900s BCE, was the first to describe the sun at the center of the solar system. But the idea wasn't fully proven mathematically until Nicolaus Copernicus (1473–1543) published his theory in 1543.

The idea was **revolutionary**. Copernicus was so worried about people being angry about his theory that he didn't publish it until he was dying.

Leonardo da Vinci died in 1519, so he never got to read Copernicus's book. But he asked many questions about the solar system and recorded his own observations. He

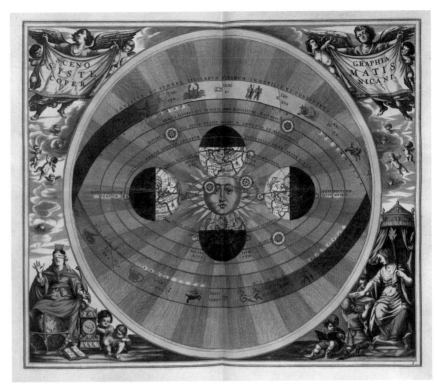

Scenography of the Copernican world system, 1661
Credit: Andreas Cellarius

used his knowledge of many different subjects to challenge what people believed about the sun and the planets. And his conclusions were grounded in science and math.

SCIENTISTS who studied the solar system used **MATHEMATICS** to understand and describe the movement of the planets.

In 1510, Leonardo wrote, "The sun does not move," in large letters on the top left of a notebook page. This was a departure from his usual style of small, reverse handwriting. The unusual lettering shows the concept was an important one—but he didn't offer any explanation about how he developed this idea. Among the other notes and sketches on this page, nothing explains why he decided the sun does not move.

He was right, of course. He also wrote that the earth was "not at the center of the universe," and again didn't provide any evidence for how he came to this conclusion. But it is clear that astronomy was an area of interest to Leonardo da Vinci.

luster: the glow of light on a reflective surface.

reflect: to redirect something that hits a surface, such as heat, light, or sound.

eclipse: when one body in space, such as the moon, passes into the shadow of another.

primary: main or most important.

compound: a mixture of two or more things.

LIGHT, OPTICS, AND THE MOON

When Leonardo studied astronomy, he connected it to his other areas of interest, just as he did with everything he studied. One important connection he made was between astronomy and the study of light and optics.

Leonardo loved thinking about how light worked. One way we know this is by looking at his paintings. To create a sense of light in his scenes, he would add small dots of white paint in the eyes or on the curved curls of people's hair. These dots made what is called **luster**, or the glow of **reflected** light.

In addition to studying light itself, Leonardo examined how light created shadows. He drew a detailed diagram of light hitting a sphere that showed how the shadows look different in different places. He also explored how light and shadows would change depending on the sizes of the light source and the object.

He wrote that if the object is "smaller than the [source of the light,] the shadow will resemble a pyramid and come to an end, as seen in **eclipses** of the moon." How does this show that Leonardo saw connections in everything he studied?

Categories of Shadows

Leonardo took a deep dive into the study of shadows. He experimented with different-size lamps and created different categories. **Primary** shadows are caused by light directly hitting an object. **Compound** shadows are caused by many sources of light. He identified shadows made by the softer lights of sunset or sunrise, shadows made by filtered light, and more. He also noticed that nearby objects can reflect light and create another kind of shadow. This study of light reflection and shadows would be important for his exploration of astronomy and in art.

At this time, people believed the moon created its own light. They also thought the moon was a perfect sphere. When they gazed at a full moon, they didn't consider that they were seeing just one part of a whole.

You can browse Leonardo's notebooks for yourself at the British Library website. What do his drawings make you think of?

🔎 British Library Leonardo

PS

Leonardo used his knowledge of geometric shapes and examined the way light reflected off of spheres. Then, he applied what he learned to the celestial object of the moon. He realized that the established experts on the solar system were wrong.

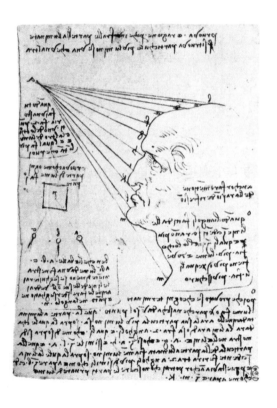

First, even though Aristotle claimed the moon and planets were perfect spheres that glowed with their own light, Leonardo could see with his own eyes that this was wrong. He didn't even need a telescope.

Leonardo realized that the sun shines on the moon and other planets and that the light we see here on Earth is sunlight bouncing off these objects and reflecting back to Earth. He wrote, "The Moon has no light of itself, but so much it as the Sun sees, it illuminates."

Once he realized that the moon was reflecting light, he knew that he was not looking at a perfect sphere. The laws of reflection mean that a perfect sphere would reflect light in a perfect circle. Any unevenness in shape, such as there is in the moon, would not create a perfect circle. There was no bright circle around the moon.

WORDS TO KNOW

oblate spheroid: a shape like a slightly flattened ball.

revelation: a surprising fact that is made known.

The moon is actually an **oblate spheroid**, which looks like a slightly flattened ball.

Because the light reflected off the moon is uneven, Leonardo also guessed the moon had an uneven surface. Have you seen photographs of the surface of the moon?

Buzz Aldrin on the surface of the moon in 1969
Credit: NASA/Neil Armstrong

Leonardo imagined that the surface of the moon was covered with a sea and that waves disrupted the light. He also guessed that there must be air on the moon to cause the waves. Both of these ideas were wrong.

But he did have two other ideas that were correct.

If you could stand on the surface of the moon and gaze back at Earth, what would you see? According to Leonardo, you'd see Earth brightly lit with reflected sunlight, just as we see the moon. This idea was ahead of its time—more than 400 years before humans got to the moon—and showed a deep understanding of the science of light.

Leonardo understood that the moon moves through space. Through his understanding of how light reflections work, he was able to draw a diagram that explained the phases of the moon. He knew we could see only the portion of the moon that was hit by sunlight.

You can see Leonardo's notes and drawings of the moon in his notebook pages at the British Library website. What do you see that you recognize as factually correct? Is there anything there we know today to be wrong?

🔎 BL Leonardo moon

PS

Leonardo also noticed it was sometimes possible to see dimly lit parts of the moon. He stated that these parts were lit by the sunlight reflected off the earth. He called it "earthshine."

His study of shadows, shapes, and light made these **revelations** possible. Leonardo constantly applied ideas from all of his interests into everything he studied.

Photo of the earth taken from *Apollo 8*, called "Earthrise," 1968

WORDS TO KNOW

lens: a curved piece of glass that focuses light passing though it to make things look clearer or bigger.

distort: to change or make something look different from its normal shape.

WHY IS THE SKY BLUE?

You might think of this question as coming mainly from younger children. It's also a question that some of the greatest human minds have tackled—including Leonardo da Vinci.

As a painter, Leonardo knew that color was essential to his work. But he did not want to simply paint a blue sky. Just as with his studies of anatomy and engineering, he wanted to understand how the sky worked and use that wisdom to better inform his art. Where did the color of the sky come from?

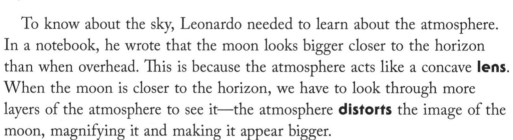

What does light have to do with the *Mona Lisa*'s smile? **Find out in this video about how Leonardo worked with light and optics to create the iconic smile.**

🔍 Atlantic Leonardo reality

To know about the sky, Leonardo needed to learn about the atmosphere. In a notebook, he wrote that the moon looks bigger closer to the horizon than when overhead. This is because the atmosphere acts like a concave **lens**. When the moon is closer to the horizon, we have to look through more layers of the atmosphere to see it—the atmosphere **distorts** the image of the moon, magnifying it and making it appear bigger.

This same concept also makes the sun look larger when it's rising or setting.

Once Leonardo understood that the atmosphere can change how things look, he realized that the sky didn't actually have a color, it just appeared that way. He wrote that the sky looked blue because of "warm humidity, evaporated in very minute . . . atoms . . . which catches solar rays."

Leonardo was describing water vapor in the atmosphere. He believed that water vapor scatters the blue light of sunlight.

While climbing Monte Rosa, a mountain in Italy, he noticed the shade of blue in the sky deepened and darkened as he climbed higher. He guessed that if he climbed higher and higher, the sky would get darker and darker. Eventually, he would leave the atmosphere and "should find darkness." In the atmosphere, there is no more water vapor to scatter the blue light. That's why when we see footage from space, there's no blue sky—there's only the darkness of space.

Make a Prism

Leonardo figured out that water vapor trapped sunlight and scattered only the blue light around the atmosphere—this is why the sky looks blue. He did several experiments to prove his idea. Leonardo also wanted to find out what causes a rainbow. The concepts—water capturing and scattering light—are connected. You can make your own rainbow at home with a prism, which is an object that disperses light and reflects it into the full color range of the rainbow. Place a small mirror in a drinking glass. Fill the glass with water. Set the glass on a white surface. Shine a flashlight on the mirror. You can also use sunlight—you may have to move the mirror around to make sure the sunlight hits it. Adjust the glass until you can see the rainbow projected onto the wall. What does it look like? Can you make it more intense? Draw your observations in your science journal.

Of course, Leonardo always tested his ideas to see if his hypothesis was right. As an experiment, he sprayed a fine mist of water in a dark chamber. The water vapor made a sunbeam look blue.

WORDS TO KNOW

gradations: small changes from one level to another, such as those that take place when painting with color.

camera obscura: a box with a hole on the outside that projects an image on a screen inside the box. The projected image appears upside down.

He also tested his idea with painting. First, he painted a canvas with various background colors, including "a most beautiful black." Then, he painted a light wash of white over each of the background colors. None of the other background colors showed a "more beautiful azure" than the black background. He was able to see that layers of paint created a more realistic representation of the way light looks. The sky is not one flat shade of blue. It has subtle **gradations**, or different intensities of blue.

TO THE EARTH

Leonardo wanted to answer big questions, such as how big is the sun? Earlier philosophers had said the "sun was the size it looks," but Leonardo doubted that.

Answering this question would not be easy. Leonardo wrote the sun's rays "strike the eye with such splendour [sic] that the eye cannot bear them." And he was right—no one should ever look directly at the sun, not because of splendor, but because you could seriously injure your eyes if you do so.

Dilating Pupils

Pupils dilate because of a reflex, which is an involuntary movement we can't control. There are a few things that can cause a pupil to dilate. One is a lot of light—another is emotion. Some chemicals also cause pupils to dilate. But we can't control the muscles in our eyes voluntarily. See for yourself! Put your face close to the mirror. Find the pupil in your eye, the black hole in the center of the iris. Are both of your pupils the same size? While you're looking in the mirror, have a friend shine the flashlight near your eye, but not close enough to touch. How does your pupil react? Remove the light. What does your eye do? Repeat this experiment in a bright room and a dim room. Does your pupil dilate more or less? Record your observations in your science notebook. What are some other reflexes that you have? Which ones are involuntary? Which ones are involuntary, but you can control sometimes?

Leonardo thought he might use a **camera obscura** to try to find the size of the sun.

The camera obscura had been around for a long time—Leonardo did not invent it. It is a large box with a hole in one side. The inside of the box is dark and the hole should be small, like a pinhole. When the viewer enters the box, the image behind the viewer is projected on to the wall inside the box, in front of the viewer. The unique thing is that the image is upside down.

Because light travels in a straight line, the light from the top of the object appears at the bottom of the projected image. The light at the bottom of the object appears at the top of the projected image. The light from the middle of the object stays in the middle.

Leonardo's painting *The Virgin, the Child, and Saint Anne* shows his expert understanding of the sky and why it is blue.

Leonardo was familiar with the camera obscura. It works the same way as the pupil of our eye. The pupil is the hole that lets in the light and the images we see are created on the back wall, or retina, of our eye. In a camera obscura, it takes a mirror to reflect the image and turn it right-side up—but humans are lucky because our brain does this for us automatically.

The Camera Obscura.

Credit: Wellcome Collection (CC BY 4.0)

A camera obscura is a safe way to view an eclipse or measure the sun without the danger of damaging your eyes. While it is not clear that Leonardo ever did extensive work on measuring the sun, he did make observations and conclusions about light waves that were accurate and important. He wrote that light rays have power, which we now call energy, and that light rays don't have physical qualities, such as weight. Plus, he was able to observe that light rays always travel in straight lines. These were advanced observations for his time.

Leonardo understood these properties of light even though scientists are still testing them in the twenty-first century. In fact, much of the work he did was on concepts that scientists today are still studying and perfecting. This includes a way of traveling that most people hadn't even imagined back during the Renaissance—flight. We'll take a look at Leonardo's work in this area in the next chapter.

ESSENTIAL QUESTION

How did Leonardo learn about space even though he could not leave Earth?

MAKE A
CAMERA OBSCURA

A camera obscura is sometimes called a pinhole camera. You can make one and use it to explore light like Leonardo.

Caution: Ask an adult to help you use the Xacto knife.

❯ **Using a sharp pencil or a pushpin, make a small hole in one of the shorter ends of the shoebox.**

❯ **In the other short end of the box, cut out a square.** An easy way to do this is to make an X with an Xacto knife. Ask an adult for help with this step. Once you have the X, you can cut out the full square.

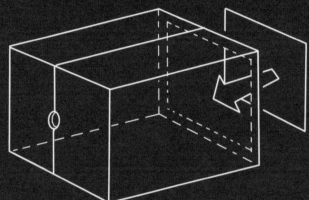

❯ **Cut a square of wax paper to cover the square.** Tape it to the box.

❯ **You've made a camera obscura!** Take the camera, lamp, and blanket into a dim room.

❯ **Turn on the lamp.** Hold your camera so the wax paper end is facing you.

❯ **Put the blanket over your head and the camera, but leave the end of the box with the pinhole uncovered.** Don't cover the pinhole with the blanket!

❯ **Face the lamp.** What do you see on the wax paper? How does it look?

❯ **You can add more details as you practice drawing in one-point perspective.** Add color if you like! What does color add to the picture?

Think Like Leo!

Find a magnifying glass and hold it in front of the pinhole. How does it change the image that you see?

TEXT TO WORLD

Find photographs of the sky at the library or online. How does the look of the sky change in different images? What kind of light offers the most realistic skies?

MAKE A
SUNDIAL

A sundial is a simple device used to measure time. By tracking the movement of a shadow created by the sun, a person can measure the passing of time. A sundial is the combination of Leonardo's studies of light and shadow.

The sundial uses a stick, called a gnomon, to create a shadow. As the sun moves through the sky, the shadow of the gnomon moves around a circle. There are many ways to make a sundial. Try this one and then brainstorm other methods!

❯ Using a pen or marker, write the number 12 on the outer edge of the plate.

❯ Using the ruler, draw a straight line from the 12 to the center of the plate.

❯ On a sunny day, go outside around noon with your paper plate, straw or stick, watch, and compass. Find a clear space in the ground that will get full sun.

❯ Use your compass to find the direction of the closest pole, either the North Pole or the South Pole. If you live north of the equator you live in the Northern Hemisphere, so you would look for north.

❯ Put your plate on the ground.

❯ Push the straw or stick, the gnomon, through the plate so it secures the plate to the ground. You can also use pushpins to secure the edges of the plate to the ground.

WORDS TO KNOW

time zone: a region where all clocks are set to the same time. There are 24 time zones in the world, each one an hour ahead of the zone to the west.

❯ Gently push your gnomon so it tilts slightly north.

❯ Exactly at noon, line up the line you drew on the plate with the shadow created by your gnomon.

❯ Go outside every hour and check the position of the shadow. It might help to set an alarm to remind you.

A sundial from Pompeii, in ancient Rome, from before 79 BCE

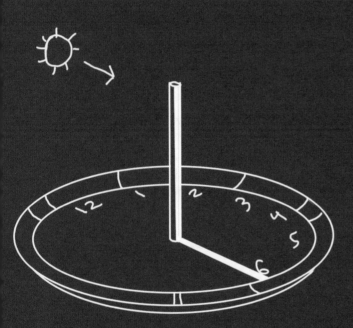

❯ **The shadow will move clockwise around the plate.** At 1 p.m., write the number 1 at the end of the first shadow. Write the number 2 at the end of the shadow at 2 p.m. Continue this until the sun sets.

❯ **Come back outside in the morning and record the numbers at the start of each hour.**

❯ **Once your sundial is complete, use it to tell time and check your answer.** Is it accurate? How can you make a different kind of sundial? How can you make a timing device that you can carry with you?

Think Like Leo!

A sundial is a great way to tell the time where you are. Could you create something that helps you measure **time zones**? How far apart would you have to place sundials in order to observe slight differences in time?

MAKE A
MOON MODEL

INVENTOR KIT
° lamp without a lampshade, about the same height as the jars
° something to elevate the balls, such as empty jars
° 4 white balls larger than the openings of the jars

Leonardo understood that the moon doesn't have an internal light. It shines with reflected sunlight. You can demonstrate this at home.

❯ **Put the lamp on a table in the center of the room.**

❯ **Picture an imaginary circle on the table around the lamp.** Put one jar on each of the four sides of the circle.

❯ **Set up the four white balls in the open mouths of jars.** These represent the different phases of the moon. Turn on the lamp. Turn off the other lights in the room so the lamp is the only source of light.

❯ **Stand back from the table and observe how the light from the lamp reflects off the white balls.** What does the ball between you and the lamp in front of you look like? What does the ball on the other side of the lamp look like?

❯ **Draw the light and dark parts of the moon in your science journal.**

❯ **You can add more details as you practice drawing in one-point perspective.** Add color if you like! What does color add to the picture?

Think Like Leo!

Place more jars and balls around the circle in between the existing jars. How does this change the light? Sketch your observations. Can you add a model of the earth to your model of the moon? Can you recreate the earthshine that Leonardo observed?

Record in your notebook how the moon looks outside. Can you identify which phase it is in tonight?

Chapter 6

TAKING
FLIGHT

WHO IS YOUR LITTLE FRIEND?

HE'S MY PET CROW, ICARUS. HE GOT TOO CLOSE TO OUR CAT, SOLIS, BUT I SAVED HIM.

BIRDS ARE AMAZING CREATURES. I'VE BEEN ENAMORED BY THEIR ABILITY TO FLY MY ENTIRE LIFE!

When he was about 50 years old, Leonardo wrote down a memory from his infancy. When he was a baby in his cradle, a large bird with long wings and a forked tail called a kite flew down to him and used its long tail to open Leonardo's mouth, moving its tail and up and down against the baby's lips.

Was this a real memory? Or a dream?

Maybe even Leonardo never knew for sure, but he loved birds all of his life. Was it because of their flying ability? Their anatomy? Their **iridescent** feathers? Whatever the reason, it's easy to imagine Leonardo watching birds. As he explored the forests, fields, and farms of his home, Leonardo watched and drew the birds he spotted. And he longed to master their secrets of flight.

ESSENTIAL QUESTION

How did Leonardo apply his observations to his designs for flying machines?

WORDS TO KNOW

iridescent: constantly changing colors that look like a rainbow.

feat: an achievement that requires great skill or strength.

moat: a deep wide ditch, filled with water, surrounding a fort or castle.

For more than 20 years, Leonardo studied birds and their flight. In fact, he produced enough material to make an entire book about this topic—the *Codex on the Flight of Birds*. It includes beautiful drawings of birds, observations about birds that most people never noticed, and incredible inventions of flying machines.

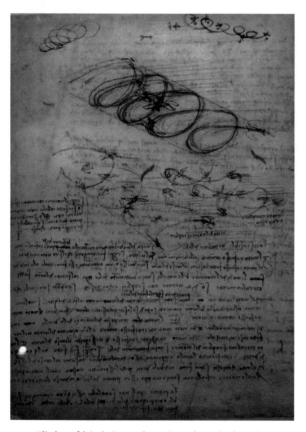

Flight of birds in and against the wind, 1505

Leonardo drew and studied many animals, including **HORSES, CATS,** and **DOGS,** but **BIRDS** seem to hold a special place in his heart. There's a famous legend about him buying caged birds at markets, sketching them, then setting them free.

WATCH CLOSELY

It's not easy to study birds. Most fly away if a person comes close! And observing a flying bird is even more challenging, especially hundreds of years ago, when humans simply didn't go very high very often.

But Leonardo was good at it. Were his eyes somehow better, sharper, than other people's eyes? Was that the secret to his success?

Not really—his secret was hard work and practice. He practiced noticing and worked diligently at the act of observation. He was patient and thorough, which meant he was able to see things that other people didn't notice. That included dragonfly wings.

This is an incredible **feat**. Dragonfly wings are transparent and almost invisible when the insect flies. Leonardo discovered that the best place to observe them was near a **moat**, so he went and watched—and watched, and watched.

"If you wish to have SOUND KNOWLEDGE of the forms of objects," Leonardo wrote, **"BEGIN WITH THE DETAILS of them, and do not go on to the second step until you have the first well fixed in memory."**

—Leonardo da Vinci

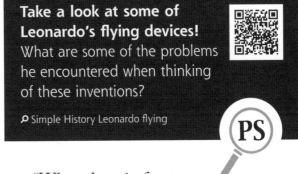

Take a look at some of Leonardo's flying devices! What are some of the problems he encountered when thinking of these inventions?

Simple History Leonardo flying

He realized that dragonflies have four wings, not just the two that are most evident at first glance. And he discovered that the wings behaved in a very specific way. "When those in front are raised those behind are lowered," he wrote.

Paper Airplanes!

Have you ever made and flown paper airplanes? It's easy and fun! Take a look at the patterns at this website. When you've done several and are feeling confident about your folding abilities, that's the time to branch out and improve on the designs. Improvise! Leonardo was a champion of improvisation. He always tried to find a way to make a technique, device, or idea better. What kinds of paper airplanes can you come up with? How far can you get one to fly?

fold n fly

The more Leonardo observed birds, the more he learned about flight. He noticed that birds of different species flap their wings differently. Some birds, such as mourning doves, move their wings faster when they flap down. Crows lower their wings more slowly than when they raise them. Magpies flap up and down at the same speed.

He also noticed the relationship between a bird's tail and flight. "Birds with short tails have wide wings," he wrote.

THEATER SHOWS

Leonardo started learning about flight while he was an apprentice in Florence. One way he was introduced to this topic was through the theater. Many artists were hired to use engineering skills to create devices that made actors fly across a stage during performances.

"When birds are descending near the ground and the head is below the tail, they lower the tail, which is spread WIDE OPEN, and take short strokes with the wings; consequently, the head is raised above the tail, and the speed is checked so that the bird can alight on the ground WITHOUT A SHOCK."

—Leonardo da Vinci

Leonardo drew some designs for wings for this purpose, though these wings were for show, not for flight. They looked like bat wings that would move up and down when a person turned a crank.

The theater might have been the reason for one of Leonardo's most famous drawings. Many people believe Leonardo da Vinci invented the first helicopter. In his notebooks, he has a drawing for an aerial screw, which looks like a spiral made of fabric hovering above a platform. The center pole of the device is a screw and as a blade traveled down the curved groove of the screw, the fabric spiral would spin and rotate.

A 3-D replica of Leonardo's aerial screw
Credit: Elliott Brown (CC BY 2.0)

But historians believe this device was not actually meant to fly. Instead, it was probably designed for a theater performance. One reason historians don't see this as a flying mechanism is because there's no person drawn in this device. In all of his other drawings of flying machines, people are shown making the machines work.

WORDS TO KNOW

species: a group of living things that are closely related and can produce young.

density: a measure of how closely packed items are.

compact: using up little space, parts are close together.

compressed: squeezed or pressed together.

pressure: a force that pushes on an object.

WIND AND WATER

In order to master the science of flight, Leonardo explored what he called "the science of the winds."

In typical Leonardo style, he connected his studies of air to his knowledge of water. Water and air have a lot in common—they both exhibit fluid characteristics—so this was a reasonable starting place. In fact, most scientists took for granted that birds stayed in the air for the same reasons that ships floated on water.

But Leonardo questioned everything. Was this true? How did birds manage that? Could humans learn useful techniques about floating from the birds in the air? Leonardo knew there were connections between air and water, but he suspected there were differences, too.

Leonardo saw the world in a way NO ONE ELSE DID.

I HOPE ONE DAY WE ARE ABLE TO LEARN HOW TO FLY.

I BELIEVE WE WILL! IF I AM UNABLE TO SOLVE THE MYSTERIES OF FLIGHT, I AM SURE ONE DAY SOMEONE ELSE WILL!

IT WOULD BE AMAZING TO BE ABLE TO FLY WITH THE BIRDS!

For one thing, birds are heavier than air, while ships are not heavier than water. That means birds can't float like ships. Gravity would pull the birds to the earth. He described gravity as the "attraction of one object to another." He knew that gravity kept the seas from falling off the planet.

Another difference between air and water is **density**. Density describes how **compact** something is or can be. Leonardo knew water could not be **compressed** as much air could be. Water is more dense than air.

Great Backyard Bird Count

The Great Backyard Bird Count is a community science program. It started in 1998. It happens during four days in February. All around the world, volunteers watch and count birds for 15 minutes. Then, they report their observations to the Cornell Laboratory of Ornithology. The scientists use the data from the bird counts to check if bird **species** are growing in number or shrinking. Scientists also learn if their ranges, or the places where species live, are growing or shrinking. They learn if species are moving from rural areas to cities. **You can join the Great Backyard Bird Count at this website!**

🔍 Great Backyard Bird Count

Leonardo envisioned a wing pushing down on air. The wing would push the air into a smaller space. As the air under the wing is compressed and forced into a smaller space, the air **pressure** against the wing increases.

The air above the wing is not compressed. So, the air pressure above the wing is lower. The higher air pressure under the wing pushes back on the wing and works to keep the bird in the air.

WORDS TO KNOW

lift: a force that pushes upward on an object in flight.

cross section: the two-dimensional shape you would see if you cut a three-dimensional object in two with one straight cut.

velocity: how fast something moves in a direction.

principle: an idea or belief.

Leonardo also understood that both the wing of the bird and the air push on each other. They exert force on each other. The forces are equal and opposite. This was an early version of the third law of motion that Isaac Newton would describe 200 years later.

Knowing that the air pushes back on the bird's wing with the same force was key. It helped Leonardo visualize the concept that we now call **lift**. This is how birds and planes stay in the air.

We know from the drawings in his notebooks that Leonardo understood that moving air has less pressure than still air. He drew a **cross section** of a bird's wing, showing how the top of the wing is curved. That curve in the wing forces air to travel a farther distance, up and over instead of straight along underneath.

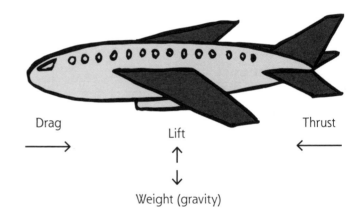

Drag

Lift

Thrust

Weight (gravity)

Three Laws of Motion

Sir Isaac Newton described his three laws of motion in 1687. The first law says an object will stay at rest or in motion in a straight line unless a force causes it to change. The second law says the **velocity** of an object changes when there is a force on it. The third law states that every action or force has an equal and opposite reaction. These laws are important to understanding the rules of flight. Although Leonardo didn't write down these laws as Newton did, he understood them and used them in his designs.

All Forces are Equal

Stronger Lift and Thrust

Stronger Drag and Weight (gravity)

The air on top of the wing has to travel faster, too. All of this means the air on the top of the wing travels faster and is less dense than the air below the wing. The air above the wing puts less pressure on the bird. The air under the wing puts more pressure on the bird. These forces work to keep the bird in the air.

Even though Leonardo described this idea, we call it the Bernoulli **principle**. This is because Daniel Bernoulli (1700–1782) published his description of this principle in 1738.

PEOPLE POWER

As he learned more about the science of how birds fly, Leonardo was soon sketching designs for machines that might actually fly. Here, he combined his knowledge of engineering, the physics of flight, and human anatomy. He used his artistic skill to sketch several versions of flying machines, from gliders to parachutes. He truly believed he could create a machine that would allow people to fly.

Force

The third law of physics says that for every action or force, there is an equal and opposite action or force. So, when a person jumps into the air and lands on the earth, they exert a force on the earth. The earth pushes back with the same force. However, the person feels it more because the mass of the earth is much greater than the mass of a person.

But his machines needed energy to get into the air. He didn't have engines or jet fuel—they hadn't been invented yet! So, he turned to people. Most of Leonardo's flying machines rely on people to power them.

Leonardo studied human anatomy to understand human muscles. He wanted to know which ones were the strongest. He calculated how much power each muscle group could possibly have and discovered that human leg muscles are the strongest. Then, he designed machines that used the strongest muscles.

The Pyramid Parachute

Even Leonardo's smallest sketches show how he used his understanding of flight. On a page in his notebook where he wrote about air pressure on an eagle's wing, he described and drew a parachute. This parachute doesn't look like modern parachutes—it has a cloth stretched over a wooden frame shaped like a pyramid. He called it a "tent of linen."

Leonardo didn't see this as a way for people to fly. Instead, it was a way to "throw himself down from any great height without sustaining injury."

You can make your own parachute!

What shape might be best for a parachute? Find out by making your own. You just need a square of light fabric, four pieces of equal-length string, and a test pilot—an action figure or animal figure. Even a paper clip would work! Tie one end of each piece of string to each of the four corners of your fabric and attach the other ends of all four strings to your test pilot. Go to a high spot that is safe to test your parachute. Hold the parachute in the center of the fabric—and drop it! How does it fall? Once you have a parachute that works, innovate! What happens if you have a heavier test pilot? What happens if you use heavier fabric? What happens if you use a larger piece of fabric?

"Study the **ANATOMY OF THE WINGS** of a bird together with the breast muscles that move those wings. Do the **SAME FOR MAN** to show the possibility that man could sustain himself in the air by the flapping of wings."

—Leonardo da Vinci

One machine that Leonardo drew in the 1480s looks almost scary. He called it his "flying ship." It is a tower of gears in a bowl with four blades for wings at the top of the tower. Perhaps these four blades were inspired by dragonflies. A person stands in a bowl and turns cranks with their arms and pushes pedals with their feet. If they go fast enough, maybe the four flapping blades at the top would lift them into the air.

However, there's no way to steer this flying ship!

Leonardo drew many versions of devices with people flapping wings like birds. He called this idea his *uccello*, which is Italian for "bird."

Even though his understanding of how to make something fly was right, his devices would never take off, simply because he was limited by the materials of his time. Anything he built would be made of leather, wood, and cloth. What do all of these have in common? They're very heavy. There wasn't a person alive strong enough to flap the wings of these heavy machines and get them into the air.

Despite his detailed plans, there's no record of any of his flying machines working.

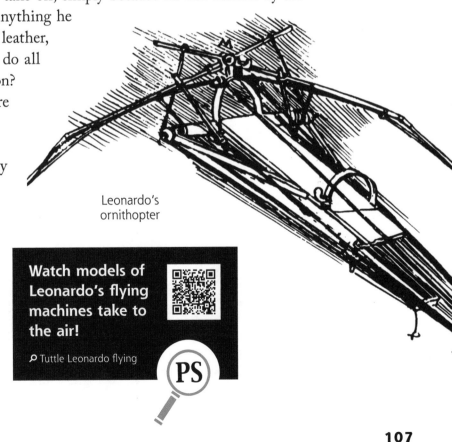

Leonardo's ornithopter

Watch models of Leonardo's flying machines take to the air!

🔍 Tuttle Leonardo flying

PS

GLIDERS

Leonardo realized in the early 1500s that birds have muscles in their chests that are much stronger than those in people. So, after he had left Milan and returned to Florence, he switched his focus from flight based on flapping wings to gliding. He called this "soaring flight."

Dream Believing

Even with the energy and materials limits that Leonardo faced when inventing flying machines, he still dreamed of testing out his designs. He even wrote down plans for trying one over a lake in case it failed. (Better to crash-land in water than on land.) He recommended wearing a "bladder," or bag inflated with air as a belt, which would act as a life preserver.

Today's system of gliding

Who Invented the Paper Airplane?

Some credit the Chinese with the creation of the first paper airplane more than 2,000 years ago. During the early 1900s, paper airplanes grew in popularity, with designs published in magazines for fun. Some of these had tabs that pushed into slots to make for sturdier construction! Engineers figured out that using paper airplanes could help them figure out which airplane designs worked best—even the Wright brothers might have used them when building the first flying machines. Modern paper airplanes were designed by Jack Northrop (1895–1981) during the 1930s. Northrop was cofounder of the Lockheed aircraft corporation. He used paper models of planes and wings to solve design problems.

Gliders have fixed wings, or wings that don't move or flap. Leonardo's devices have a platform or harness that holds a person. These gliders follow the same principles of flight that Leonardo had previously explored, but they would not stay in the air indefinitely because they had no power source.

People are built very differently from birds. One main difference is that BIRD BONES ARE HOLLOW, which makes them lighter.

Despite the limitations of his flying machines, one thing that never stayed grounded was Leonardo's imagination. Leonardo da Vinci was unique. His endless curiosity and imagination helped him see things that other people overlooked—such as birds' wings. He found answers to questions other people never even asked!

ESSENTIAL QUESTION

How did Leonardo apply his observations to his designs for flying machines?

What made Leonardo da Vinci really special was his willingness to ask questions and explore new ideas, even if he wasn't sure they would work. He wasn't afraid of being wrong or asking "what if?" and "why?" As you encounter new ideas, keep asking questions and thinking, just like Leonardo!

BUILD A
PAPER HELICOPTER

INVENTOR KIT
° paper
° paper clip
° paper helicopter design

Leonardo invented an ornithopter, not a helicopter. This paper helicopter is inspired by nature, as are many of Leonardo's designs. It mimics the motion of a maple seed. Take a look!

❯ **Draw or trace this paper helicopter design on a piece of paper.**

❯ **Cut out along the solid lines.** Fold on the dotted lines.

❯ **Slide the paper clip over the bottom.**

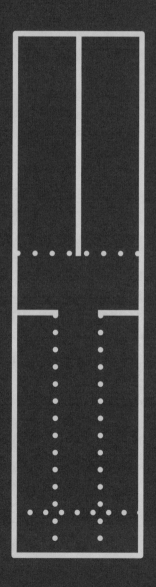

TEXT TO **WORLD**

What human designs can you spot in your home that were inspired by nature?

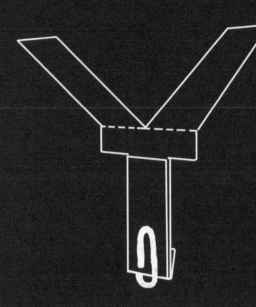

> **Try throwing the paper helicopter into the air.** How does it fall? Is it fast or slow? Does it fall straight down or does it fall in a curve?

> **Try dropping the paper helicopter from a height.** Does it fall differently than when you threw it in the air? Is it fast or slow? Does it fall straight down or does it fall in a curve?

Think Like Leo!

How do you think the paper helicopter works? What if you added more paper clips? Would that change how the helicopter falls? What if you made the blades larger?

The Line Trick

Leonardo was a master of observing the world. Here's a game he loved to play with friends. It also helped him improve his observation skills.

> Have a friend draw a line on a paper and hang it on a wall.

> Bring some friends into the room and have them stand a good distance away from the wall. Start with at least 10 feet.

> Ask your friends to cut a straw the same length as the line on the wall without moving any closer.

What happens? Does anyone get it right? Try again and let people stand closer to the wall. How close do they need to be for everyone to get it right? Try the game again and ask people to stand farther back. How far back do they need to go for everyone to be wrong? What does this tell you about perception?

TEST THE
THIRD LAW OF MOTION

Leonardo understood the third law of motion even though he never published his studies. Try this classic experiment to demonstrate the third law of motion.

❯ **Thread the string through the straw.**

❯ **Tie the string between two objects, such as the backs of two chairs.** Make sure the path is level and horizontal and the string is tight.

❯ **Inflate the balloon, but don't tie it closed.** Hold it closed with one hand while you tape the top of the balloon to the straw. The balloon should hang below the string.

❯ **Move the balloon and straw to one end of the string.** This is your starting line.

❯ **Release the balloon.** What direction does it travel? Record your observations in your science notebook.

Think Like Leo!

What happens if you inflate the balloon with less air? What happens if you inflate a bigger balloon? How does friction affect the balloon?

TRY THIS!

❯ **Fold a piece of tape in a circle so it sticks to both a toy car and a balloon.** Inflate a balloon and secure it to the car.

❯ **Release the balloon.**

✱ What direction does the car move? Why?

✱ Why does the car slow down?

✱ Could you get a block or object without wheels to move using a balloon?

✱ Don't forget to record what you observe in your notebook!

abacus: a device for counting and calculating.

acuity: sharp, clear vision.

aerial: relating to the air.

algebra: using letters and symbols to represent numbers and amounts in equations and formulas.

altitude: the height of an object above sea level. Also called elevation.

ambidextrous: able to use the right and left hands equally well.

anatomy: the study of the bodies of humans, animals, and other living things.

anisocoria: a condition in which the pupils in someone's eyes are different sizes.

aorta: the main artery in the body.

apprentice: a person who works with a master to learn a skill or trade.

Archimedes' screw: a simple machine used to pump water uphill. A screw is inside a cylinder or tube. The bottom goes into the water. A handle turns the screw and carries the water up a slope.

arithmetic: basic math functions, including addition, subtraction, multiplication, and division.

arteriosclerosis: the hardening of artery walls, especially in old age.

arteries: blood vessels with muscles in their walls that carry blood from the heart.

astrology: studying the movements of stars and planets and claiming they influence human actions and behaviors.

astronomy: the study of the sun, moon, stars, planets, and space.

atmosphere: the layer of gases surrounding a planet.

automaton: a moving mechanical device that imitates a human.

blood vessel: a thin tube in an animal's body that carries blood.

botany: the study of plants.

camera obscura: a box with a hole on the outside that projects an image on a screen inside the box. The projected image appears upside down.

CE: put after a date, CE stands for Common Era and counts up from zero. BCE stands for Before the Common Era and counts down to zero. These are non-religious terms that correspond to AD and BC. This book was printed in 2021 CE.

chord: a group of three or more musical notes played together.

circulatory system: the body system that carries blood and other fluids around the human body. It includes the heart, blood, and blood vessels.

circumference: the distance around a circle.

clergy: a priest, monk, minister, or other person ordained by the church.

compact: using up little space, parts are close together.

compound: a mixture of two or more things.

compressed: squeezed or pressed together.

concave: a surface that curves inward, like the inside of a sphere.

conservation of volume: the concept that a substance, such as a liquid, stays the same quantity even if its appearance or shape changes.

contract: to shrink or make smaller.

convex: a rounded shape like the outside of a bowl.

cross section: the two-dimensional shape you would see if you cut a three-dimensional object in two with one straight cut.

density: a measure of how closely packed items are.

depth: how deep something is, or the measurement that gives a shape three-dimensional (3-D) qualities.

device: a piece of equipment, such as a phone, that is made for a specific purpose.

diagram: a simple drawing that shows how something looks and how it works.

dilate: to become wider, more open.

dimension: when an object looks like it has length, width, and depth.

displace: to replace fluid with an object. The weight of the water that is moved is equal to the weight of the object.

dissect: to cut something apart to study what is inside.

distort: to change or make something look different from its normal shape.

ducat: a gold coin used during the Renaissance in Europe.

eclipse: when one body in space, such as the moon, passes into the shadow of another.

eliminate: to get rid of.

emotion: a strong feeling about something or someone.

engineer: someone who uses math, science, and creativity to solve problems or meet human needs.

engineering: the use of science, math, and creativity in the design and construction of things.

engineering design: the process engineers use to identify problems and come up with solutions.

exterior: on the outside of something.

feat: an achievement that requires great skill or strength.

fluid: a substance that can flow and take the shape of its container.

force: a push or pull on an object.

forgery: a copy, not the original.

fossil: the remains of any living thing, including animals and plants, that have been preserved in rock.

friction: the resistance caused when one object or surface moves against another.

geocentric: a model of the universe, now disproved, that the earth is the center of the solar system.

geometry: a branch of mathematics that deals with points, lines, and shapes and where they are in space.

golden ratio: when two numbers have a ratio that is the same as the ratio of their sum to the larger of the two quantities.

gradations: small changes from one level to another, such as those that take place when painting with color.

gravity: the force that attracts one thing to another.

hatch marks: lines drawn close together to create areas of shadow in a drawing.

heliocentric: a model of the universe in which the planets orbit the sun and the moon orbits the earth.

hoist: a device that works with a pulley to lift heavy loads.

horizon: the line where earth and sky appear to meet.

humanism: a belief that human beings can improve themselves and their world through a rational approach to problem-solving.

hypotenuse: the longest side of a right triangle, opposite the right angle.

illegitimate: born of parents not married to each other.

improvise: inventing or creating something while you're doing it.

innovation: a new invention or way of doing something.

interior: on the inside of something.

invested: to be deeply involved and interested.

iridescent: constantly changing colors that look like a rainbow.

larynx: an organ in the throat that holds the vocal chords. Also called the voice box.

lens: a curved piece of glass that focuses light passing though it to make things look clearer or bigger.

lift: a force that pushes upward on an object in flight.

linear perspective: a way of drawing so that some things look closer to the viewer and some look farther away.

luster: the glow of light on a reflective surface.

lyre: a stringed instrument, like a u-shaped harp.

mathematician: someone who studies mathematics, or numbers.

medium: the type of materials used to make art, such as paint or clay.

membrane: a thin layer or boundary in an organ or living thing.

methodical: using a system or following steps to do something.

Middle Ages: the period of time between the end of the Roman Empire and the beginning of the Renaissance, from about 350 to 1450 CE. It is also called the Medieval Era.

mirror writing: backward writing that goes from right to left.

moat: a deep wide ditch, filled with water, surrounding a fort or castle.

monk: a man who lives in a religious community and devotes himself to prayer.

movable type: an important advance in printing where individual characters could be rearranged easily, allowing books to be printed more cheaply.

mural: a painting done directly on a wall.

notary: a person who handles legal papers such as contracts and deeds.

oblate spheroid: a shape like a slightly flattened ball.

optics: the study of the properties and behavior of light.

orbit: the path of an object circling another in space.

organ: a part of an organism that has a specific job, such as the heart or stomach.

organism: something living, such as a plant or an animal.

perfectionist: someone who wants everything to be done in a certain way and who isn't satisfied with outcomes that don't match expectations.

perpetual: never stopping.

perspective: a skill used in drawing to give the correct view of objects in a painting, using their height, width, and position to each other. It can be used to create a sense of distance.

physicist: a scientist who studies physical forces, including matter, energy, and motion, and how these forces interact with each other.

physics: the study of physical forces, including matter, energy, and motion, and how these forces interact with each other.

pi: the number represented by the symbol π and often shortened to 3.14.

pigment: a substance mixed with oil or egg yolk to create colored paint.

pitch: how high or low a sound is, depending on its frequency.

plane: a flat surface.

Platonic shapes: a set of five shapes, all of which have faces that are regular polygons of the same size and all the vertices (corners) are identical. Also known as Platonic slides.

polygon: a geometric figure with at least three straight sides and angles.

polyhedron: a solid in three dimensions with flat polygonal faces, straight edges, and sharp vertices.

polymath: a person with a lot of knowledge across many different subjects.

portrait: a painting of a person showing only the head or head and shoulders.

portray: to describe or depict someone or something.

precise: exact, very accurate.

pressure: a force that pushes on an object.

priest: a member of the clergy in Christianity who leads religious services and performs rites.

primary: main or most important.

principle: an idea or belief.

printing press: a machine that presses inked type onto paper.

process: an activity that takes several steps to complete.

projectile: a solid object that it is sent flying through the air, such as a rock or arrow.

proportion: the balanced relationships between parts of a whole.

prosperous: financially successful, wealthy.

pulley: a simple machine consisting of a wheel with a grooved rim that a rope or chain is pulled through to help lift a load.

pupil: the dark opening in the center of the eye.

ratio: the comparison of two numbers to each other.

reflect: to redirect something that hits a surface, such as heat, light, or sound.

Renaissance: the period in European history between the 1300s and 1700, which was marked by dramatic social, political, artistic, and scientific change.

retina: the part of the eye containing light-sensitive cells that send electrical signals to the visual area of the brain for processing.

resistance: a force that slows down another force.

revelation: a surprising fact that is made known.

revolution: one complete turn made by something moving in a circle around a fixed point.

revolutionary: markedly new or introducing radical change.

scholar: a person who studies a subject for a long time and knows a lot about it.

scroll: a piece of paper or parchment with writing on it that is rolled up into the shape of a tube.

sculpture: a carving of stone or metal.

sfumato: a painting technique that blends colors and tones together without clear outlines, a smokiness.

simple machine: a device with few or no moving parts. It performs work by changing motion and force. There are six main kinds: inclined plane, lever, wedge, wheel and axle, pulley, and screw.

slope: a surface that has one end higher than the other end.

solar system: the sun and eight planets that revolve around it.

species: a group of living things that are closely related and can produce young.

sphere: a round, solid figure, a ball.

spinal cord: a bundle of nerves in the spine that connects the body with the brain.

spire: a pointed roof, such as on a tower.

spiritual: relating to the mind and spirit instead of the physical world.

sternocleidomastoid: a muscle that is connected to the chest bone and clavicle and attaches to the skull. It bends, rotates, and flexes the head.

suspension: to hang something in the air free on all sides except at the place where it is supported.

technology: the tools, methods, and systems used to solve a problem or do work.

tempera: paint made by mixing pigments or colors with egg yolk.

tempering: to bind something together, as with pigment and egg yolk.

tendon: flexible cords that attach muscles to bones.

tension: a force that pulls or stretches an object.

theoretical: based on an idea or concept, not based on a real experience.

three-dimensional (3-D): something that appears solid and can be measured in three directions, length, width, and depth.

time zone: a region where all clocks are set to the same time. There are 24 time zones in the world, each one an hour ahead of the zone to the west.

understatement: a statement that makes something seem less important that it truly is.

valve: a device that controls the flow of liquid through a pipe or tube.

vanishing point: the point at which something grows smaller and smaller and almost disappears completely.

veins: blood vessels without muscles in their walls that carry blood to the heart.

vellum: fine paper made from the skin of a calf.

velocity: how fast something moves in a direction.

ventricle: a hollow part of an organ.

vertebra: one of the small bones that form the backbone. Plural is vertebrae.

vertex: a meeting point where two lines form an angle. Plural is vertices.

vibrate: to move back and forth or side to side very quickly.

viola organista: a musical instrument invented by Leonardo da Vinci. By pressing on keys, a moving belt made certain strings vibrate and produce sound.

volume: the amount of space an object takes up or the amount of space inside an object.

water vapor: the gas form of water in the air.

will: a legal document that explains what happens to a person's belongings when they die.

zibaldone: one of Leonardo's notebooks, or a collection of different kinds of things.

Metric Conversions

Use this chart to find the metric equivalents to the English measurements in this book. If you need to know a half measurement, divide by two. If you need to know twice the measurement, multiply by two. How do you find a quarter measurement? How do you find three times the measurement?

English	Metric
1 inch	2.5 centimeters
1 foot	30.5 centimeters
1 yard	0.9 meter
1 mile	1.6 kilometers
1 pound	0.5 kilogram
1 teaspoon	5 milliliters
1 tablespoon	15 milliliters
1 cup	237 milliliters

ESSENTIAL QUESTIONS

Introduction: Why was the Renaissance a time of great art, invention, and discovery?

Chapter 1: How did Leonardo's view of the world influence his paintings and drawings?

Chapter 2: How does understanding the parts of a machine help you understand how the machine works?

Chapter 3: How did Leonardo apply what he learned about the human body to his other areas of study?

Chapter 4: How did Leonardo's artistic skills help him with mathematics?

Chapter 5: How did Leonardo learn about space even though he could not leave Earth?

Chapter 6: How did Leonardo apply his observations to his designs for flying machines?

BOOKS

Cox, Michael. *Leonardo Da Vinci: Stroke of Genius*. Scholastic, 2019.

Edwards, Roberta. *Who Was Leonardo da Vinci?* Penguin Workshop, 2005.

Krensky, Stephen. *DK Life Stories Leonardo da Vinci*. DK Children, 2020.

Olinger, Heidi. *Leonardo's Science Workshop: Invent, Create, and Make STEAM Projects Like a Genius*. Rockport Publishers, 2019.

WEBSITES

Smithsonian Air and Space
airandspace.si.edu/exhibitions/codex

National Geographic Kids
kids.nationalgeographic.com/explore/history/leonardo-da-vinci

Museum of Science
mos.org/leonardo/node/1

MUSEUMS

Leonardo da Vinci Interactive Museum
mostredileonardo.com/en

Museo de Leonardo da Vinci
museoleonardodavincifirenze.com

Royal Collection Trust
rct.uk/collection/themes/exhibitions/leonardo-da-vinci-a-life-in-drawing/the-queens-gallery-palace-of

MOVIES

Being Leonardo da Vinci. Image Hunters, 2019.

Leonardo: The Works. 2019 exhibitiononscreen.com/films/leonardo-the-works

Decoding Da Vinci. NOVA, 2020. thirteen.org/programs/nova/decoding-da-vinci-93ssvo

SELECTED BIBLIOGRAPHY
Books

Capra, Fritjof. *Learning from Leonardo: Decoding the Notebooks of a Genius*. BK Currents Book, 2013.

Capra, Fritjof. *The Science of Leonardo: Inside the Mind of the Great Genius of the Renaissance*. Doubleday, 2007.

Da Vinci, Leonardo. *The Da Vinci Notebooks*. Time Warner Book Group, 2006.

Da Vinci, Leonardo. *Leonardo's Notebooks: Writing and Art of the Great Master*. Black Dog & Leventhal, 2013.

Da Vinci, Leonardo. *Leonardo da Vinci on the Human Body: The Anatomical, Physiological, and Embryological Drawings of Leonardo da Vinci*. Gramercy Books, 2003.

Isaacson, Walter. *Leonardo da Vinci*. Simon and Schuster, 2017.

Kemp, Martin. *Leonardo da Vinci: The 100 Milestones*. Sterling, 2019.

Kemp, Martin. *Leonardo Da Vinci: Experience, Experiment, and Design*. Princeton University Press, 2006.

Krull, Kathleen. *Leonardo da Vinci*. 2005.

Malam, John. *Tell Me About LDV*. Carolrhoda Books, 1998.

McCurdy, Edward. *The Mind of Leonardo da Vinci*. Dover Publications, 2005.

Pedretti, Carlo. *Leonardo da Vinci: The Complete Works*. David and Charles Publishing, 2006.

Videos

Leonardo's Dream Machines. PBS Home Video, 2005.

Leonardo da Vinci. Kultur International Films, 2006.

QR CODE GLOSSARY

Page 7: pbs.org/video/how-did-leonardo-da-vinci-paint-mona-lisa-w4ra4r

Page 17: theguardian.com/artanddesign/2019/may/26/leonardo-life-in-drawing-review-royal-collection-queens-gallery

Page 19: qz.com/quartzy/1569706/leonardo-da-vincis-only-surviving-sculpture-unveiled-in-italy

Page 32: youtube.com/watch?v=Hnge32B0RDs

Page 34: thekidshouldseethis.com/post/how-to-make-leonardo-da-vincis-self-supporting-arch-bridge

Page 35: ca.news.yahoo.com/da-vinci-contraptions-brought-life-bruges-exhibition-100135994.html?guccounter=1&guce_referrer=aHR0cHM 6Ly93d3cuZ29vZ2xlLmNvbS8&guce_referrer_sig=AQAAALv4Rdnf_ jbXXz3qbtBNIKfCr3gzt86QRjyVvN3MeIE5_BMpG-oRPGL2uX7JBFisgDh YClGX1pk0vSSMA2NeV1hpRoZZZQ52lmi3S2MyKgXN8N50jozh-y7WB-vy93CO93gJ-Za338EAMITK-XYsCzaHMMIeWLRs4vXNvoBAU10n

Page 37: youtube.com/watch?v=3h5oBb9O-dw

Page 46: youtube.com/watch?v=J9xUL5Yi_8M

Page 51: nytimes.com/video/science/100000003892113/the-hummingbirds-tongue.html

Page 52: bbc.com/news/health-28054468

Page 61: youtube.com/watch?v=MmPTTFff44k

Page 68: youtube.com/watch?v=aMsaFP3kgqQ

Page 78: youtube.com/watch?v=MwsGULCvMBk

Page 85: bl.uk/manuscripts/Viewer.aspx?ref=arundel_ms_263_f001r

Page 86: blogs.bl.uk/digitisedmanuscripts/2018/01/leonardo-da-vinci-on-the-moon.html?utm_source=feedburner&utm_medium=feed&utm_camp aign=Feed%3A+digitisedmanuscripts+%28Medieval+Manuscripts%29

Page 88: theatlantic.com/video/index/542025/leonardo-da-vinci-augmented-reality-mona-lisa

Page 99: youtube.com/watch?v=Y0_htkvCVpE

Page 100: foldnfly.com/#/1-1-1-1-1-1-1-1-2

Page 103: earthsky.org/earth/register-participate-great-backyard-bird-count

Page 107: youtube.com/watch?v=nu6ZGMDeiUI